W9-AIA-278

Dear Homefolks

Dear Homefolks

A Doughboy's
Letters and Diaries

by

Roy Evans Thompson
an American soldier
from 1917 to 1920, World War I

Compiled by Dale Thompson

REGENT PRESS
BERKELEY, CALIFORNIA

Copyright © 2009 by Dale Thompson

ISBN 13: 978-1-58790-154-6
ISBN 10: 1-58790-154-4
LCCN: 2008926160

SUBJECT CLASSIFICATIONS

1. World War I — Military life

2. World War I — Medicine

3. Medicine — World War I

FRONT COVER: DESIGNED BY
ROY'S DAUGHTER
MARJORIE THOMPSON BURGESON

Printed in The United States of America
REGENT PRESS
2747 Regent Street
Berkeley, CA 94705
regentpress@mindspring.com
www.regentpress.net

For

*Roy Evans Thompson, my father, who,
without ever talking about it,
demonstrated to me a work ethic
and love of accomplishment
that I deeply appreciate.*

Acknowledgements

I am grateful to my father, Roy Evans Thompson, for his pack-rat gene, without which this story could not have been told. The letters, pictures and other bits and pieces were securely preserved from World War I until his death in 1978. My parents moved often during their life together. I know of at least 19 permanent residences between 1925 and 1978. I am grateful that on at least 19 occasions they did not yield to temptation to discard that box full of old army stuff.

Roy's letters and diaries are the bulk and the basis of this work. They are his words, as reported by this 21, 22, 23 year old soldier who had a 9th grade education. Some of the photographs are from his box of mementos, others collected elsewhere.

Besides the letters, my father left a packet of assignments that he wrote for an English class in the pre-college / continuation high school he attended after the war before entering Washington State College in 1921. In one of these assignments, titled Autobiography, *he reviews the first 25 years of his life and articulates his reverence for education and his academic aspirations.*

I wish to thank my sister, Marjorie Thompson Burgeson, my wife, Rosemary Grandine Thompson, and a multitude of friends and family, including Marcy Thompson, Barbara Morgan, Michael Hanlon and Bill Hyman for their support, encouragement, and editing skills as this project took shape.

— Dale Thompson
Richmond, California
March 13, 2008

Contents

PHOTOGRAPHS AND MAPS

PROLOGUE

    Family

    Harvest crew and combine

CHAPTER 1

    Draft Registration Card

    Draft Registration Card, back

    A typical envelope

    Camp Lewis, under construction

    Doughboy barracks

    Letter, KC stationery

Prologue

This book tells the story of a doughboy, a common soldier, in World War I. It is mostly my father's words recording his two year encounter with the Great War. He entered the army as a young farmer and part-time auto mechanic. During his twenty-seven months as a soldier he started on the path that led to his becoming a professional mechanical engineer, a patent holder, and a champion of continuing education.

ROY EVANS THOMPSON was born in 1896 at Albion, in the state of Washington. His family lived on a wheat farm, which they farmed with horses. Southeastern Washington, the area surrounding Pullman and Colfax, is known as the "Palouse Country". The village of Albion lies between these two towns.

Roy was the second of seven children. His father, George, became blind about the time Roy was born, which meant that his mother, Cora, became George's eyes in the management of the farm. At a very early age the children worked with their father; he provided the muscle and guidance and they provided the sight. Roy finished eighth grade, and following common practice in the early 20th century in agrarian America, never expected to attend high school. As the oldest son, it was assumed that Roy would take over running the farm. He became a capable farmer and was good with horses, but he never loved horses as his father did. Roy learned carpentry by building and repairing farm buildings. At about age 14, he and his father built a barn that stood for eighty years. But his greatest enjoyment at this time was operating and maintaining the farm's machinery. When automobiles first arrived

The George A. Thompson Family
Albion, Washington, November 1917
TOP ROW: Lloyd, Clara, Vella, Mamie, Roy
BOTTOM ROW: Dorma, George, Cora, Leola

*in the area, he wanted to learn everything he could about them.
Sometime between 1910 and 1914 he got a winter job in a local
automobile repair shop. Here he learned that his schooling was
inadequate for him to understand the intricacies of automotive
electrical systems. Determined to get more education, he enrolled
in high school, while continuing to work on the farm and at the
auto shop, completing one year of study.*

*The United States entered World War I in April 1917, and in No-
vember of that year, at the age of 21, Roy was drafted into the army.*

*The bulk of this story is made up of letters written by Roy be-
tween the ages of 21 and 23 (November 1917 to July 1919). The
first letter was written a few days after he entered the army and
they continue until he went home on leave from Letterman General
Army Hospital in San Francisco in July, 1919. Roy's discharge papers and records from Washington confirm that he was discharged
from the Army at San Francisco, on January 28, 1920.*

Roy's letters and diaries often refer to the weather. Sometimes

Roy Thompson working as "header operator" on this wheat combine, 1915. It used 33 horses and 5 men. (Roy has X near his hat.)
[Photo donated by George Brigham, eldest son of Vella Thompson Brigham]

it may seem he was at a loss for material to write. Another possibility is that, with his background, it was the stuff of daily conversation on the farm. The well-being of the crops, the garden and the livestock were all dependent on weather.

These letters were saved by Roy's mother, and later by Roy. His children were unaware they existed until after his death in 1978 when they were discovered among his effects. From the letters, it is evident a few are missing; yet those remaining record a compelling chapter from a soldier's life.

After the war, he enrolled and attended for one year an accelerated high school program at Washington State College. This qualified him for entrance into college in the fall of 1921. Some of his English papers from that program have survived. One of them is a theme, titled Autobiography. *With this seven-page, hand-written document, Roy reveals his insight and attitude toward education, an attitude that shaped the rest of his life and the lives of his children. A copy is included in the Addendum.*

Roy was a private person, who rarely spoke of his army experiences. The only army connected story I recall was his observation that since the army does everything in alphabetical order, if

*he were to serve again, he would change his name to Aaron Ab-
bot. This would place him close enough to the head of the line to
receive warm food and clothes that fit.*

*The early letters portray a man who had probably never been
a hundred miles from home until the army sent him off to western
Washington, Texas, Georgia, New Jersey and finally to France,
then brought him home by way of New York, Chicago and California. A defining incident in his 27 months in the army was his
involvement in a railway accident in January of 1919, at Gondrecourt, France, resulting in the loss of his right foot.*

*Sixty-seven of his letters and postcards survived, along with
two small pocket calendars that he used as diaries. There were
also several photographs. Fortunately for the continuity of this
story, he recorded in the diaries the names and locations of the
army camps and towns and hospitals in France where he was stationed or had passed through. This chronological list, to be found
in the Addendum with a map, lists the locations in France that, in
the letters, were always left blank for reasons of security.*

*We have here the story of a young man who went to war. My
father was faithful in his letter writing, a master of understate-
ment, and always careful to thank his family for their letters and
packages. Roy apparently always guarded his words to minimize
his family's anxiety over his personal safety. One letter reports
that during the Atlantic crossing to France, "We had a fine trip;
I wasn't sick at all. We had splendid weather the last few days;
warm clear days and moonlight nights. Nothing exciting occurred
during the whole trip". His diary entries tell another story, mentioning seasickness, submarine drills, sleeping fully clothed while
in the submarine zone, rough seas, cruiser escorts, perfect submarine weather, and finally, salt water showers.*

*Through his attention to detail, we know the names of the
ships he took to and from France. Research confirms that his regiment sailed to France on the U.S.S. President Lincoln, a ship that
was torpedoed and sunk three months later.*

Strangely, with the exception of "drilling" there is no mention of the basic training that became common during and since WWII. From the time he reported for duty on November 4, 1917, until he was on the ground in France (February 26, 1918), only 114 days elapsed.

The history of U.S. Army operations during WWI reveals that during the crush to expand the army and get soldiers to France, the basic plan was to transport the troops to France and to rely on the French and English for assistance with their basic training for trench warfare. Roy's lack of basic training may be explained by the Army's immediate and critical need for experienced auto/ truck mechanics.

Included among his papers was a certificate, promoting him to sergeant. It is dated 1 January 1918, just seven weeks after reporting for active duty.

Here is the record he left...

— *Dale Thompson*
(son of Roy E. Thompson)
Compiled 2004-2008

Adventures of an Inductee

We begin in 1917 at the local draft board in Whitman County, Washington. Roy Thompson was 21 and therefore qualified for the first draft enrollment of World War I. We know nothing about his attitude towards the war, draft legislation, registration for the draft or induction into the army. Line 12 of the REGISTRATION CARD shows that he considered deferment to be a possibility. His clear and characteristic signature appears virtually the same here as it did throughout his life.

The war in Europe, which Americans have come to call "World War I", started in June 1914 at Sarajevo, Bosnia, with the assassination of Archduke Ferdinand of Austria-Hungary. The United States remained neutral until April 6, 1917. Historians agree that the sinking of the Lusitiana, a British passenger liner, in May 1915, was the tipping point that drew the United States into the war. Among the 1198 people who died in that incident were 128 Americans. It took the United States another 23 months to declare war and join France, England and Italy against Germany and her allies, known as the "Central Powers".

In 1914 the United States had a standing army of about 135,000 men. By November 11, 1918, the U.S. Army had over 2,000,000 men in France.

The War Department, anticipating that Congress would eventually declare war, developed the mechanics of a military draft well before the declaration of war in April 1917. A month elapsed before Congress, on May 18, 1917, approved a conscription bill.

June 5, 1917 was set aside as the day for the first national draft. Roy's draft registration card (see facing page) was obtained from the National Archives.

Roy was inducted on November 4, 1917, at Colfax, Washington. From there he proceeded directly by train to Camp Lewis, Washington, a military post between Tacoma and Olympia, about 300 miles from his home.

His letters begin at Fort Lewis. These were written on very thin paper, usually in ink. The stationery, whatever the origin, was quite uniform, 5-1/4" wide x 8-3/8" high. The envelopes were 5-5/8" wide x 4-3/8".

CAMP LEWIS, SATURDAY AFTERNOON
[NOVEMBER 10, 1917]

Dear Everybody,

Well, I'm going to write a little bigger letter than I did last time, as we have Saturday and Wednesday afternoons off, and I have a little time. They're fitting us up in shoes this afternoon. Just got into a pair of 8-1/2 EE. They're sure some shoes. I can take them out into the promenade ground and "Right Face" and "Left Face" without moving the shoes. They make tracks about fourteen inches wide.

Ben left for Mineola, N.Y. this morning and Harry goes this afternoon. Don't suppose I'll get to go to the train as they're making us stick pretty close to barrack this afternoon. We just signed up a card, giving our age and occupation. They called for stenographers and cooks the day after we landed, also shoemakers. They called for carpenters yesterday noon. I volunteered and worked on a garage for one of the officers yesterday afternoon and this morning. He wants us to come back Monday.

REGISTRATION CARD

Form 1   No. 23

		Age, in yrs.
1	Name in full _Roy Evans Thompson_ (Given name) (Family name)	21

2 Home address _____ (No.) _____ (Street), _Albion_ (City), _Wash._ (State)

3 Date of birth _March_ (Month) _22_ (Day) _1896_ (Year)

4 Are you (1) a natural-born citizen, (2) a naturalized citizen, (3) an alien, (4) or have you declared your intention (specify which)? _Natural born._

5 Where were you born? _Albion_ (Town) _Wash._ (State) _U.S.A._ (Nation)

6 If not a citizen, of what country are you a citizen or subject? _____

7 What is your present trade, occupation, or office? _Farm Laborer_

8 By whom employed? _Father_
   Where employed? _Near Albion_

9 Have you a father, mother, wife, child under 12, or a sister or brother under 12, solely dependent on you for support (specify which)? _No_

10 Married or single (which)? _Single_   Race (specify which)? _Caucasian_

11 What military service have you had? Rank _____; branch _____;
   years _____; Nation or State _No._,

12 Do you claim exemption from draft (specify grounds)? _Does work for a Blind Father_

   I affirm that I have verified above answers and that they are true.

   Roy E. Thompson.
   (Signature or mark)

CA 1 (If person is of African descent, tear off this corner.)

World War I Draft Registration Card
From National Archives – SE Region

A lot of the boys went to Tacoma. There's a football game between the Army and the Marines today.

This place is laid out in blocks like a town. Two barracks to the block, and common streets between. There are 212 Barracks, so when you remember the Y.M.C.A. buildings, warehouses, hospitals, stables, exchanges, headquarters buildings etc., you will

Draft Registration Card, back

realize that we have some town.

The barrack buildings are wood, two stories high, about 40 or 45 feet wide by 140 or 150 long. The upper floor and about 1/2 of the lower are bedrooms, the rest kitchen, dining room, supply rooms, offices, etc.

The feed is good. For dinner today we had wieners, kraut, potatoes, macaroni with tomatoes, bread and pudding. For breakfast we had mush, potatoes, toast and syrup. We usually have meat for breakfast, but not always. Yesterday for dinner we had fish instead of meat. The bread we have is good. We've had only one or two messes of cornbread yet; light bread the rest of the time. We have coffee for breakfast, water for dinner, tea for supper. We generally get fruit in some form once a day. The feed is good, plenty and well-cooked, and that is all we expect.

I've been called out twice since I started this letter. The first time I was awarded hat, gloves, 3 pr. sox, and a belt, and the next time an overcoat. I'll ship my suitcase and clothes back as soon as I get the rest of my outfit. Don't be surprised if it comes collect, for I'm going to go easy with my money till I get some pay. Some of the boys that came in the first draft haven't seen any money yet, and that's been about two months. So you can pay the express and sell the duds to square it.

I saw Wiley last night. He got in Wednesday. I looked for him on the train, and after I got in here, but didn't see him until Harry told me where he was. Did Joe and John enlist? If they did, get me their address and send it as soon as you hear where they are. I heard they are going to examine the rest of the registered men the 15th. Do you know if it is so? How is the old jitney and did my prescription fix the tires? There are cars and trucks running in all directions here all the time. Also lots of army wagons and some motorcycles.

Write and tell me all the news and I'll write again when I can think of something to say.

As ever,
— Roy
Corrected address
44th Co. 166 Depot Brigade
Camp Lewis, Wash.

[No Date on the letter, postmarked: Nov 15, 1917]

Dear Home Folks,

Got your letter day before yesterday, and Leola's just a few minutes ago. I intended to write yesterday, but didn't get around to it. Went up to the "Y" *[Y.M.C.A.]* last night to write, but couldn't get in sight of a table, so mailed some clothes, talked around a while, and came back to the barrack. When I got in it was too late to write, as lights go out at nine o'clock.

They kept us going this morning. Took us out to drill at 7:00. Stayed a couple of hours, and came in to move our bunks so that 90 more men could move in with us. Then went back to drill and stayed until 11:30.

The drill is very amusing. They'll get us all lined up, marching straight ahead and tell us to "Squads Right", and when we get turned we're all out of step and out of place in the line, and straggling around like a bunch of wild geese.

We didn't do so bad until this morning, as they drill us first in squads (8 men each) then platoons (3 squads). This morning they put us in company formation. There must have been 120 to 150 of us, so our individual mistakes just showed up so much worse. They'll march us out in a column, four abreast, then we'll make a turn at right angles, and march off abreast, two deep. They sure produce some line after they turn. It would make a snake ashamed of itself. We won't have to drill this afternoon, as this is Wednesday.

A bunch of the boys are singing a parody on "Massa's in the Cold, Cold Ground". They sing it "All de Germans are a-weepin', The Kaiser's in de cold, cold ground". Another one of their favorites is, "Oh, where do we go from here?"

To return to the subject of drill: They generally give us a little run at double time to warm us up in the morning, then they'll march us around a while, and then give us half or three-quarters

A Typical Envelope

of an hour of physical exercises, mainly to develop the lungs and legs, tho of course they aim to develop us all over.

The Y.M.C.A. is doing a great deal of good among the boys here. There are two of their buildings within easy reach of here. I go to one or the other nearly every night. They furnish us, light, warm rooms to read, write or visit in, and the environment there is considerably better than in the barracks. They have quite a library and loan the books out free, keep current newspapers and magazines on the tables and furnish the boys free stationery and a place to write. They also sell apples, candy, post-cards, stamps, etc., but do so merely to accommodate the boys, and not for financial benefit. So you can see what they want with the $35,000,000. I think they'll make good use of it.

The people that run these barracks go pretty strong on neatness and order. They send a squad all around the building every morning to pick up burned matches, cigarette stubs, etc. from the building to the middle of the street on each side. So you can imagine this is a neat place.

We signed up our vocational cards yesterday, giving our experience at different kinds of work. I'm going down to see the captain pretty soon, to put in an application for transfer, but don't expect to get it, as there is lots of demand for the kind of job I want.

Mama, did you see the kits the Red Cross gave the Colfax boys? They're a khaki bag about 7 X 10 inches, with shoe-string drawstrings at the top. If its not too much trouble I wish you'd make me one. I need something to put my toothbrush and paste, shaving set, and other trinkets in after I send the suitcase home. They (the gov't) furnish a big bag for clothes. Did Mamie get over the grippe? Write when you can and I will write when I can think of anything to say.

— Roy

CAMP LEWIS WASH.
NOV. 21, 1917

Dear Home Folks,

Had a chance today to get a good little picture of the camp, so I'm sending you one. It's taken from the other side, so our barrack doesn't look very big. It's just like the others tho, so it doesn't matter. It's the farthest one back in the row I marked. We have the best location I know of. The infirmary is next door, it is only one block to a fine exchange.

I have been carpentering again today. About twelve or fifteen of us were putting the time building an addition to the kitchen. Our tool equipment consisted of two hammers (both insults to the name) a hand saw, which was worse than the one at home usually is; a home-made wooden square, and two dull axes. It was sure a treat to see two or three guys putting up lattice work with a 5 lb. axe.

But we have the promise of some tools and a week of carpenter work. I drifted from the picture somewhat, so I'll discuss it some more. The open ground is, of course, the parade ground. If you'd

Camp Lewis, Washington…..Under construction, 1917

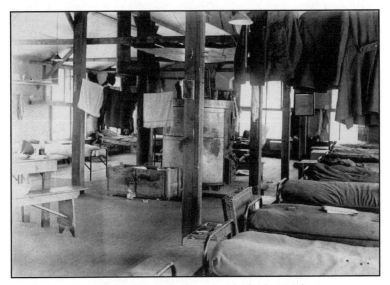

Doughboy barracks—not ready for inspection
Camp Holabird, Maryland
Photo by Harry Williams
[Donated by Neil Rozeman, Strongsville, Ohio (great-nephew of photographer)]

get out there on a clear day you could see from a few hundred to a few thousand men out there drilling. I say clear day, because often you can't see across the parade ground for the fog. Do you notice how the trees look in the background? They generally look just about that dim and hazy when they're over half a mile away.

There are about the same number of buildings on each side, and they are still building more. So this picture doesn't show nearly all of them.

Each barrack will hold 250 men, so quite an army can be housed here. Right back of my barrack is another railroad, and back of that are the stables, and a large flat; this is used for trench practice.

20,000 men paraded yesterday before Gen. Greme, but I was in bed, and too lazy to get up to see it. I felt pretty bum the last three or four days; had tonsillitis, but am much better now. The California boys had to take tonsillitis, and a lot of us caught if from them.

This seems to about finish me up, but I'm writing to Vella yet.

So long, Everybody,

— Roy

I think the picture will look fine on my shanty wall next winter, don't you?

[POSTMARKED NOV 25, 1917]
CAMP LEWIS, TUESDAY
[Nov. 20, 1917]

Dear Home Folks,

Got your letter this evening and was very glad to hear from you, as I always am. I got a letter from Clara today; also one from Mamie. Joe hunted me up last Sunday morning. I hadn't known before that he was here, but he came here the day before I did. We visited an hour or two. He seems like a very nice fellow. He told me that Orla was to be married soon; probably would have been ere this if he hadn't gone to Juliatta.

I am still carpentering; have about another day of it, I think. I have only been on the drill field twice for over a week. Gen. Irons reviewed the Brigade yesterday afternoon and again this afternoon, and I had to go out then. I suppose I will have to drill again about Friday. Thursday will be a holiday unless we are billed out of here. If we are, we may have to drill, holiday or no holiday. But I don't expect to drill, so am figuring on going to Tacoma for Thursday afternoon and night.

The boys out of here for Texas expect to leave Thursday or Friday. I could have been in as well as not if I'd known in time which ropes to pull, but I didn't get wise until too late. At least if I get in now it will be a miracle.

We signed up the allotment cards this evening. It's a statement about your age, family, etc., and how much money you want them to have. Then the government sends them money and you never see it. There will be another card concerning insurance and other matters later on. I am going to send $15 a month home if I can get it allotted. I think I will take out some insurance too. The rate for my age will be between $6 and $7 per $1000.

It rained quite a little last night, the first for about a week. Several showers to-day, and its been raining cats and dogs for about four hours. The ground around the barrack is almost a sheet of water. I wish you had some of it. Well, it's 8:40 and I must wash my teeth and bathe and get into bed by 9. (I don't have to, but the lights go out then.) so I must quit. I got the watch fine and dandy Sunday. It is considerably admired, especially the protected crystal.

— Roy

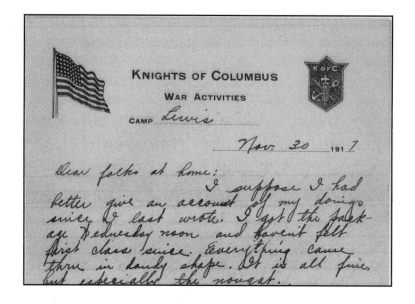

CAMP LEWIS
Nov 30, 1917

Dear folks at home:

I suppose I had better give an account of my doings since I last wrote. I got the package Wednesday noon and haven't felt first class since. Everything came thru in dandy shape. It is all fine, especially the nougat.

The boys all say they had one of the finest dinners here that they ever saw. They had 215 lbs of turkey, and I don't suppose there were over 150 to 180 men here. They had pie, cake, oranges, bananas, nuts, ice cream, and I don't know what all else.

I went to Tacoma yesterday morning, intending to get dinner at a restaurant and go to Lodge at 1:00pm. About 11:00 I went up to the Y.M.C.A. to kill time and a fellow there grabbed me and invited me out to dinner. Everybody that was willing to take a soldier to Thanksgiving dinner left their name and address at the

Y.M.C.A. and as many men would be sent out as they wanted to feed. But this fellow was there in person and I promised to go out to dinner. I went out a little later. It was a long ways out, but well worth the hike. I had as fine a dinner as I ever ate anywhere, and what is more, it was in a house, and a fellow could eat like a gentleman (which they don't do in camp.) They fed us all the turkey and pie we could eat, and filled the corners with fruit, nuts and candy. There were three of us there, and we were certainly treated like princes. One of the fellows was from Montana and the other from California. Both of them seemed to be nice fellows. I left about four o'clock and went down to lodge. They took me out to supper, and the Lord knows I didn't need it; and after supper they held another session. I got out to camp at 12:30. And when I got there I found another box of candy, so I don't expect to feel normal for another week at least (but don't let that discourage you if you want to repeat the dose.)

I had to go back to drilling today, but I don't like it as well as carpenter work. I make four bits every day tho, so I should worry.

We have had a nice day to-day, but the three days preceding it simply poured. Dad, don't you ever talk to me any more about the gentle coast rains in which you can work all day without getting wet. That dope is all a dream.

The bunch for Texas leave Monday. I don't see any chance to go, but I'm going to have another try at it to-morrow. It won't hurt anything if it does no good.

Don't let the raisins worry you. I can get them within a hundred yards of the barrack just as cheap as you can buy them there. I can also get apples, not like you sent, but very good at 2 for 5¢. Barring a slight overindulgence in sweets, I'm feeling fine now. Thank you very much for everything. It sure "hit the spot". How do you like this stationery? Another guy and myself were in there looking around and we grabbed some paper just for the fun. They are doing about the same as the Y.M.C.A.

— Roy

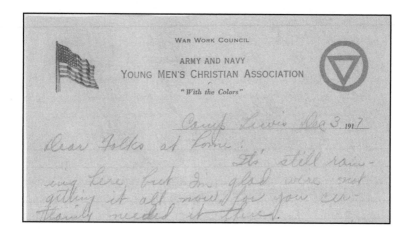

CAMP LEWIS
DEC 3, 1917

Dear Folks at Home,

It's still raining here, but I'm glad we're not getting it all now for you certainly needed it there.

I just got thru looking at the movies, "The House of a Thousand Candles" was on at the "Y" to-night but it wasn't nearly as good as the book. It was horribly butchered up. It's the first time I've been there, tho they have a show 2 or 3 times a week.

I saw Bill Nolin last night. He's been here about a month. He told me he'd been married for two years. He was drafted from Southwestern Wash., where he's been teaching. I was sure surprised to see him.

I applied for a transfer to a telegraph company Sat. I'm going to keep on until I get something, if such a thing can be done. I rather think I'm on a trail now but there is nothing certain about it. The company I applied for last is, as I understand it, a company to build and maintain telegraph lines. They are going to operate 7 Dodges, 27 motorcycles and about 40 Jeffrey Quad Trucks. I don't remember the exact number. I picked them because they're just forming and also because they have Dodges, and I can almost claim to be an expert there.

I got a letter from Jess to-day. Well it's nearly bed time, and I must beat it to the barrack. I'll let you know if anything happens. Just finished my package today, except butter and preserves. Everything was sure fine.

— Roy

KELLY FIELD NO. 1
[NEAR SAN ANTONIO, TEXAS]
DEC. 14, 1917

To my numerous relatives:

How are you all by this time? I'm feeling fine as ever, as are all of us since we got our feet dry once more.

We're living in tents here. Big round ones with six beds and a stove in each. One of the fellows I room with is from Hay, one from Sunset, one from Idaho Falls, one from Montana (he is a W S C Mining Eng. Man) and I don't know where the other fellow is from. They are a good bunch, and all from <u>44.</u>

Men are coming in here fast; new rows of tents going up every day. Lots of men are from New York and Columbus, Ohio, but I imagine every state is represented. Most of the men are enlisted, and they haven't much use for us, but we don't worry about that any. It won't be long until no discrimination will be made anywhere, for after the enlistment stops, we'll all be mixed up everywhere.

I have no idea how long we'll be here. We get a trade test sometime. Some boys have got theirs in less than a week, and some have been here a month and haven't rec'd it yet. I suppose we'll know what our job will be after that. I think I can land something here.

We've been having nice dry weather. Freezes a little nights, but hasn't been very warm or very cold since we've been here. They had a bad sandstorm here last Friday.

I haven't seen Joe yet, don't know whether he's still here or not. I'm going to hunt for him this evening some more.

More next time.

— Roy

Postmark: Dec 17, 1917
10:30 PM, San Antonio, Tex

[A post card……Text says] " Hello Ma: - What do you think of this picture? This is the way we do it, only we don't have the tub or the washboard or the clothesline or the pins. Write me (use full name) San Antonio, Tex. Gen. Del. I expect to move any time and the mail service here is bum."

Kelly Field
Dec. 20

Dear Everybody,

How goes it with you? We are having fine weather. It was clear and bright yesterday and is again to-day, but was a little cold last night.

I got my trade test Sat. afternoon. I went in as Engine Apprentice and I think I made it all right. Yesterday morning they called out 230 of us from various parts of camp, all mechanics, and put us in a different row of tents. I hear we leave here at 8 a.m. to-morrow. But I don't know for certain when we will go, or where,

The "campaign hat" shown on this card was replaced by early 1918 when it became evident that the flat-folding "overseas cap" solved the problem of storage presented by the larger hats.

'I'm some Laundress' postcard back.

but we all think we're going to school some where. This is a very nice place to winter but I would like to get to school some where for a while.

I'll let you know when I find out some more about it.

Did you get the box of stuff I sent? How much of it can you

name? The red objects are, according to the best information I can get, called "cactus fruit". They grow on a cactus with broad, flat spiny leaves. I think it is prickly pear. If you'll plant them you should raise some fine plants. Make the dirt half sand and don't water them much, they're not used to it.

I found all that stuff close to the camp. The seeds were in some kind of fruit. It had dried up so it was impossible to tell what they had been. There were four seeds in each. I thot perhaps they were persimmons. I guess Dad can tell by the seeds. The ground is almost covered with these little shells (where the cattle have not mashed them.) We found a few pecans, but no good ones. What the cattle here live on is a mystery to me. Dry thistles would be choice feed compared with what grows here. I think I'll go to San Antonio tonight if I can get away. I hear it's some town, and I'd ought to go see it when its only six miles away.

I was on guard duty a few nights back. It was the same as on the train as to hours; two on and four off for 24 hrs, but I had to walk "in a military manner" and keep an *empty* five-inch field gun on my shoulder in exactly the correct position. My shoulders are still sore, and I'll always have more sympathy for a plow horse in future.

I guess I had better quit. Our officers are cooking up some kind of dark plot now, and I suppose they'll spring it pretty soon.

Later in the evg. I was interrupted by being called out to stand in line for an hour. The Lieut. said we would leave at 1 p.m. to-morrow (Friday) but would not tell us where. I'll prob. Find out to-mor. And let you know. Tell Dad to send his letter along.

— Roy

I haven't got a letter since at C.L. *[Camp Lewis]*

The mystery of an army document of promotion without the individual's serial number is solved in Roy's letter of January 10, 1918, where he says, "To-morrow we each get a number..." Another military mystery is Roy's promotion from Private to Sergeant within two months of being inducted.

CAMP HANCOCK, GA.
JAN 1, 1918

My Dear Mother,

I'm going to spoil my record by writing you an individual letter, and if you don't want to let the rest of the bunch read it you don't have to.

This is a very pretty day, clear and cold. At least, it's rather cold for this country. It's thawing in the sunlight and freezing in the shade now, and it's 2:30 in the afternoon and won't be any warmer. The last two nights have been quite cold. The paper prophesied 10° weather, and I think we have had it. We had a nice little snow storm yesterday morning; lasted a couple of hours. It hasn't nearly all melted yet. I have plenty of clothing to keep me warm, but all the boys haven't. I don't think anybody is suffering tho.

The quarantine was lifted this morning, and as soon as we are examined, we can get a pass to town if no more measles is found. Everybody is feeling better over it already.

We are getting more shots in the arm to-day. I haven't got mine yet because they do everything alphabetically in the army, and I'm almost at the end of the row. If I ever enlist again my name is going to be Aaron Abbott or something of that kind so I won't have to wait in line all day. The records of our shots at Camp Lewis are lost in some way, so as to be sure we'll have to take them all over. The Captain is in the same boat. He'll make it hot for somebody, but of course that won't help us any.

I am transferred again, or rather I will be soon. The orders came this morning for a bunch of us, but they haven't been read yet, so don't know where I go, but think it will be to a different company in this regiment. I will try to find out before I mail this.

I haven't got a letter yet, but I'm expecting one to-morrow. One of my pals, Harley Soin of Rosalia, telegraphed home the same time I did, and he got two letters this morning. So some ought to be coming my way soon.

I sent to town for my money yesterday, and then the officer didn't go, and I haven't got it yet. Guess I'll manage to get it now that the quarantine is lifted.

I've run out of anything to say, so guess its time to quit. Don't be surprised if you don't get a letter for a month or more, for I don't suppose they'll let us write for several days before we sail, but I'll write as often as I can. I haven't heard anything more about when we leave, and don't suppose I will until they tell me to pack up.

Lots of love from your gallant little soldier.

— Roy

Later – haven't been informed concerning my new address. Let come as usual, and I'll get it all right.

SAME PLACE, JAN 10
[CAMP, HANCOCK]

Dear Everybody:

Still I am here and don't know yet when I will leave. We are still drawing a little clothing and marking our stuff. The company and regiment numbers and initials have to be stenciled on everything. To-morrow we each get a number and that goes on our stuff, too.

Our insurance is to be finished in the morning. I sent in my application for $10,000 to-day. It will cost me $6.50 per month. My first beneficiary is Geo. A. and my second is Cora E. I will receive in foreign service, not less than $33 per month. At my present rating (which I think is higher than I am fitted to hold) I will draw $33. I allotted $15 home, for I don't think they will pay us much overseas anyway, and you had just as well have it. I don't expect to hold the $44 rating, but if I do I think I will either allot you more or take out a Liberty Bond. Have you any corrections or suggestions to make? If you have, I imagine I can change things, but I thot this was the best arrangement I could make.

Did you hear anything about the land? What did Wilbur do with the shack? I wrote the sergeant at C.L. *[Camp Lewis]* to send the paper giving notice of allowance of filing. Did you get it?

I sent my apron home the other night. I suppose you have it ere this. I am inclosing the receipt. I insured it for $25, so if you don't get it, put in a kick. I'm also sending the case. I don't know whether the stuff is worth sending or not, but guess it is. They told us the other night to pack our cases and stack them in the office. So we tagged them and sent them collect, which was the only thing we could do.

I got some mail last night; a Testament from Rev. Newell. I suppose you know all about, tho. Also found out that the crazy mail orderly in Co. U. had my name on his list as Ray, so he's been sending it back to the P.O. as dead mail. I went to the office, and they told me that if they found any of it, they would send it to me. I suppose you'll be getting some of it soon. As usual, I couldn't find the receipt when I wanted it, but guess it doesn't matter.

Taps has sounded and I must put my candle out.

— Roy

During January 1918, Roy began keeping a diary which, except for March and into April is complete until mid 1919. These brief entries tell a slightly different story than his letters home.

DIARY

Fri. Jan 11 1918
Rain in morning. Clothing detail all day.
Windstorm about 8:30. Had to hold our
tents up for an hour. Wind blew all night.

SAT. 12
Clear and cold. Special guard duty. Went
to Augusta in evening.

SUN 13
Clear and cold; some wind. Stenciled
shelter halves and blankets afternoon
and evening. Walker moved out.

MON 14
Cool; breeze all day. Everybody moved
according to height. Hike in afternoon.
Wind and rain at night.

Tue 15
Batt.[allion] drill in morning. Inspection after dinner. Ghost walked at night. Usual weather.

Wed 16
Weather cloudy; still, warm. Drill in morning. Constructed squads for boat afternoon. Gassed at 5 p.m. Got my express.

Thur. 17
Warm still weather. Guard duty until 3 p.m. Regimental inspection afterwards. Went to town but too late to do any good.

Fri. 18
Same weather. Inspection of packs in morning. Bath, lecture afternoon. Went to Disgusta at 4 p.m.

Sat. 19
Nice warm day. On fatigue duty but nothing much doing.

[Postmark: AUGUSTA, GA. HANCOCK BRANCH Jan 22, 1:30 am 1918]
CAMP HANCOCK
SATURDAY NIGHT *[JANUARY 19, 1918]*

Dear Home folks,
        This is the end of a beautiful day. It was rather cold last night,

but has been warm and bright to-day. Lots of the boys laundered this afternoon. I tried a little of it myself but don't know how it will look when it gets dry.

I bought an emblem ring when I was in town last Sat. night. Had it sized and engraved and went in last night and got it. It is a handsome little rig. *["rig" here is Roy's humor...In the letter it is clearly written "rig".]*

I had my name and lodge number put in it, and am going to send the watch home to-morrow. (Also, the picture). I hate to part with them, but they are not necessary and I have no place to carry them. I saw that I was certain to ruin my good watch if I carried it on my wrist, so bought an Ingersoll wrist watch. Everybody says that no watch, no matter how good, will keep good time when carried on the wrist, and I believe it. I have swung axes, picks and shovels, handled heavy goods cases, and all that kind of stuff, and I saw that so good a watch has no business on my wrist. I don't like to do it when the boys gave it to me to bring along, but I think they will understand. The ring will serve for identification just as well. I have looked around a good deal and I can't find any place to carry the picture. I can carry post card size in my money belt, but no larger. We have to take, besides what we wear: extra woolen suit, 2 suits underwear, 4 pr heavy sox, "monkey breeches", 2 pr. shoes, overcoat, slicker, extra gloves, half tent, pole and pins, mess kit, canteen, towels, shaving outfit, handkerchiefs, soap, extra flannel shirt, and small articles too numerous to mention. Also three blankets. We have each a barrack bag (about the size of a

---

Masonic Lodge
Roy refers here and throughout his letters to meetings and his affiliation with the Masonic Lodge. He had joined the Masons in Albion, and these early letters sound as though the lodge organization was important to him. None of his family recalls him attending a meeting after the war, and certainly not in the last 50 years of his life.

sugar sack or a little smaller) which must not weigh over 50 lbs. The rest of our equipment must go into our pack. Do you understand why I don't want anything unnecessary?

I got two letters Thursday night; one from Maude and one from Jess. Friday morning I went to the Dead Letter Office and found five letters and a postal. Friday night I got three more. Ten letters in 24 hours is pretty good, don't you think? The express package is about used up; guess it will be finished to-morrow. It cost me 65¢ to wire for it, and 88¢ express, but it was worth lots more than that. I killed 90¢ worth of supper last night, besides the candy, ice cream, etc., I consumed. Soldiers eat everything they can get hold of when they get to town. It's one form of amusement.

Sunday. Just had dinner. Got my chevrons to-day but haven't worn them yet. It's raining again today.

Well, I guess that's all today. Tell Clara not to be sore if she doesn't get a letter, for I've lost her address.

Love to all of you,   — *Roy*

DIARY

Sun. 20
Went to "Y" and wrote letters and stayed
to church. Warm and showery. Nothing
doing.

Mon. 21
Sleet storm afternoon and night.
Batallion inspection. Stamped holsters.

Tues. 22
Clear cool day. Got up at 4:45 and packed
our stuff. Cold lunch at noon, sandwich
at 9p.m. Stood around all day. Got on
train at 11:00 p.m.

Wed 23
Clear warm day. Traveling north thru
Georgia and Carolinas.

Thur 24
Fine weather. Worked in kitchen.
Went thru Washington, Philadelphia,
Baltimore and several more.

Fri 25
Snowing in the morning, bright later.
Woke up in Jersey City. Got to Camp Merritt
at 11 a.m. Laundered all afternoon.

Sat 26
Still cool day. Nothing doing. Snowing at
night.

Sun 27
Still cool day. Room orderly duty. Wrote
letters.

Mon. 28
Snowstorm in morn. 4-mile hike after
breakfast. Movies and gym stunts at "Y".

Tue 29
Warm and still. Hike in morning. Feeling
bum.

Wed 30
Same weather. Room orderly again.
Signed payroll. T.R. at Y.M.C.A.

Thur 31
Nice still day. Mustered regiment in
morning. Insped. After. Went to N.Y. after
reveille. [See letter of Feb. 1, this must mean the next
morning]

FRIDAY EVENING
[DIARY CONFIRMS THIS WAS FEB 1, 1918]

Dear Everybody,

Just got back from N.Y. about an hour ago. Yesterday morning I asked for a pass to the town near here (*Tenafly*) and when the pass came it was made out for 24 hours, so I beat it for New York yesterday at 5:30. Took the taxi to Tenafly, interurban to Hoboken, ferry to New York, Subway uptown. Returning, elevated to 125th St., surface car to ferry, across the Hudson, interurban to Tenafly and back to camp. All I lacked was an airplane and I would have had the complete series. She's some little old town. I didn't have time to get acquainted with over half the people there.

I took time to have my picture taken by the thirty minute process. The full length picture is not bad, but I don't like the other one. However, under the circumstances, I had to do the best I could. You may divide them up as you see fit. I thot perhaps some of the kids would want them. If so, let them go <u>after you have all you want.</u> See? I've mailed all direct that I care about, so it's up to you now. I didn't send any to Clara or Mamie. More (News I mean, not pictures) next time.

— Roy

DIARY

Fri., Feb. 1, 1918
In N.Y. all day. Got back at 7:00 o'clock.
Nice day.

Sat 2
Still cool day. Worked in kitchen, but
feeling bum.

Sun 3
Warm day. Snowing in morning. Feeling
bum, in bed all afternoon.

Mon 4
Cooler and windy. Hike in morning.
Packed barrack bags. Cold night.

Tue 5
Very cold and strong wind. Carried our
bags to Creskill Station.

Wed 6
Not quite so cold. Drill in the morning.
Warmer and snowing in evening. Warm
night.

Thur 7
Warm bright day. Snow melting and
slushy. Room orderly duty. Washed
windows and wrote letters all afternoon.
Supper at Merritt Hall and more letters.

CAMP MERRITT *[NEW JERSEY]*
[FEB 4, '18]

Dear Homefolks,

Don't remember when I wrote, but I guess it's time for another one. The note I wrote Friday night wasn't worth counting. I got put on K.P. Saturday, but it was just luck and not due to the fact that I went to town. A lot of the fellows were either A.W.O.L. or overstayed their time from several hours to a couple of days. The ones that have been tried were reduced to rank of private and given 10 days K.P.

I felt bum Saturday and worse yesterday. Started a letter in the morning but never finished it. I feel much better to-day. No, I wasn't drunk; just a little too much metropolitan chow, I guess, and the resultant indigestion.

We are packing up our stuff in the morning so I presume we're about thru with this camp. We got the new issue caps a few days ago. Have you seen pictures of them? They can be pulled down so they are almost like the helmets. They are all right for bad weather.

We signed the payroll last week, and rumor has it that the ghost will walk to-day or to-morrow. It is about time; I am a good ways from broke, but running to town so much has flattened me somewhat financially, and a little more dough before I cross won't be unwelcome.

We've never found out yet exactly what we will draw. In the infantry "buck" private draws $30, 1st class private $33, a corporal $36 sergeant $40 and 1st class sergt. $51. If we draw the same I'll get $18.50 after the allotment is taken out. I am rated technical sergeant. I don't know whether I ever told you or not. I haven't said much about it, because I think it is a higher rating than I am entitled to, to begin with, at any rate. Some think we will draw more than infantry of the same rank, but it is not certain either way.

I got your letter Saturday, written the 16th, was very glad to hear Mamie was able to go back to work. I suppose she is all right by this time.

Mother, you said something about knitting me some stuff. I drew 5 pairs of heavy wool sox and 3 pairs of light wool; bought some gloves in town and drew a pair of wristlets and a sleeveless sweater from the Red Cross. So I have every thing I could use except a helmet and a muffler. It takes 15 days for a letter to go thru and I don't expect to be in this camp that long. So anything you could send probably wouldn't reach me before the last of March or April, and I wouldn't have much use for it then. If you have anything made I would advise you to either turn it over to the Red Cross or keep it. I don't really believe it could reach me in time to do me any good this winter. But I appreciate it, just the same.

I think I told you I heard T.R. *[Teddy Roosevelt]* speak at the Y. one night last week. It was pretty good. He came out strong for universal training and I believe if we had had it before the war there would not have been any war, so far as we are concerned.

I'll try to write again while I'm on this side.

Love to all of you,

— Roy

CAMP MERRITT, FEB 7 *[1918]*

Dear Homefolks:

This is a beautiful day; just like spring. The sun is warm and bright and the snow is melting. The trucks around here are throwing water about thirty feet each way, just like we did last winter the day I took mother joyriding and got stuck in a snowdrift.

There doesn't seem to be much to write; there is nothing doing here, and hasn't been. We had another hike this morning; about four miles. I am room orderly again to-day; have to keep the floor clean and the fires going, but it's a light job.

Things look like we are about thru with this camp. I am going to write another letter telling some things that I can't write in this one, but it won't be mailed for several days yet. This will perhaps be the last letter I will be allowed to mail from here. But I have told you that several times before, haven't I?

One of the officers gave us a talk yesterday about the mail service from the other side; told us what we would be allowed to talk about and what not (it is mostly not). So my letters will probably read, "I am well and hope you are the same."

I must cut this one short, for I have about a dozen more to write. Got a letter from Jess to-day.

— Roy
Co. 13, 1st M.M. Regt, S.C.
A.E.F. via New York

CAMP MERRITT, *[N.J.]* FEB 7 *[1918]*

Dear Everybody at Home:

This is my last night in this camp and perhaps the last on U.S. soil for a few months to come. I'll be in France when you get this, as it is to be held at the port until the news of our arrival is cabled back.

We are to get up at three in the morning, pack our stuff, eat breakfast, clean up the quarters and be ready to move at five o'clock, so we will have to go some.

These letters are to be collected at 8:30, and I have only a few minutes to write in. One of the fellows was discharged to-day. I hated to lose him, but was glad to see him get home, as he has a family. His rank was the same as mine, and he drew pay at rate of $46 so I guess I will get the same. That, with 10% raise, will be some better than $30, anyway.

I have nothing in particular to write more than I have already said, and I can hardly write sense to-night, anyway. I would write each of you a letter if I had time, but I absolutely haven't, so Good-by, each and everyone of you.

I'll write as soon as I possibly can, and I know you'll continue writing.

Good-bye, and love to all of you.   — Roy

P.S. – Tell me if you have to pay any postage on this. I can't find out if it has to be stamped or not.

                                                      — Roy

DIARY

Fri, Feb 8
Colder day, but not so stormy. Got up at 3, packed stuff, ready to move at 5:30 Marched to Creskill; on train at 8:30. Marched thru Hoboken at 12:00 went on board U.S.S. President Lincoln. Ready for anything.

Sat 9
Got up at 8:00, but no breakfast. Cold snowy rain all day. Boat left dock at 4 p.m. Everybody, including myself, has a headache due to overcrowding and poor ventilation.

Sun 10
Cold still day. Anchored in harbor all
day. Ships all around us. Left port about
7:00 p.m. Submarine drill in afternoon.

Mon 11
Cool clear still day. Water smooth, and
fine view. Physical drill 9:30, Sub drill
2:00. Feeling slightly under the weather,
but able to navigate. Lights out at 4:30,
much to our disgust.

Tue 12
In the Gulf Stream. Warm fine day, good
breeze; sea rougher than yesterday. A few
are sick. I have been known to feel better.

Wed 13
Clear day, high wind and rather rough
sea. Ship pitching a good deal. Ate supper,
but no breakfast or dinner. Not sick but
feeling rather bum, headache all day.

OUT ON THE ATLANTIC
[POSSIBLY FEB 13 FROM DIARY NOTE ON SEA CONDITION]

Dear Homefolks:
Well, I'm out in the middle of the big water, and still able
to handle my meals as usual. I think this fact is due to the good
weather, as we have only had one day that was very rough. I have

been feeling somewhat shaky, and have had a headache a good deal, but haven't been disabled yet.

We are getting good chow, better than we had in camp, but not quite so much of it. But we're getting more than we need at that, considering the work we're doing.

You said you had two of my pictures left. I don't know whether I told you to give Kerrs one or not, but do so if you haven't. I sent Minnie one that I had taken in New York, so you don't need to send her any. That will still leave one or two on your hands, I am not particular what you do with them. Ralph B. or some of the other kids might want one; if not, send it to some of my relation.

You also asked about my uniform. I guess the pictures will answer that. I now have 2 uniforms, 3 suits underwear, 5 pr. Sox, 3 pr. Shoes, hat, cap, overcoat, 3 pr. Leggings, 2 flannel shirts, and small articles too numerous to mention. Also sweater, wristlets, and sox from the Red Cross. I manage to keep moderately warm.

The boys have lots of fun here. Just had about an hour's argument about various sections of the U.S. They blow about their home towns like a bunch of real estate agents. Personally, I haven't seen anything that looked better than Wash. yet.

I think I told you about the way the Red Cross treated us in Philadelphia. At the port where we embarked they were at the pier with hot coffee and sandwiches. The boys sure appreciate it, too.

The old boat is dancing a jig today. Getting the wind broadside and rolling a good deal, but it doesn't bother us much yet, except when we try to walk on deck. Then we never know just where we'll stop.

I can't think of anything interesting that I'm allowed to tell, so guess I'll quit.

Lots of love,   — Roy

[notation by censor]

O.K.

R.M.Gilson

Capt. Inf. R.C.

http://freepages.military.rootsweb.com/~cacunithistories/
USS President Lincoln.html

U.S.S. President Lincoln…. Roy was among the 3,300 men of the 1st Motor Mech. Regt. Signal Corps who sailed from New York to St. Nazaire, France February 10 to 24, 1918. On May 31, 1918 this ship was torpedoed and sunk about 500 miles off the French coast while on a return trip to the U.S.

1. Home, Albion, Washington
2. Camp Lewis Tacoma, Washington
3. Kelly Field #1, San Antonio, Texas
4. Camp Hancock, Agusta, Georgia
5. Camp Merritt, New Jersey
6. New York City
7. Letterman Army Hospital, San Francisco, California

Roy's U.S. Travels 1917-1919

DIARY

Feb 21
Fine warm spring day. Cold salt bath and exercise in morning. Got into war zone, ordered to sleep with clothes on. Clear moonlight night.

Feb 22
Fine clear day. Met convoy and cruiser turned back. Big feed. Warm moonlight night and smooth sea. Ideal weather for subs. No drills. Med inspection.

Feb 26   Clear warm day. Got off boat about 9:30 marched to camp. K.P. at breakfast. Guard at camp.

That was the last diary entry until mid-April.

Chapter 2

France and the Life of a Mechanic

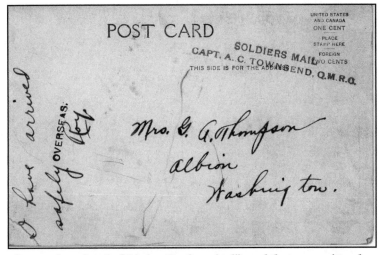

Postcard, undated: This is a "safe arrival" card that was written by each soldier before embarking. After the ship arrived in France and a cable was received in the U.S.A. confirming safe arrival in France, the postal group mailed the cards. Capt. Townsend devised and ran the military mail operation in Hoboken, NJ.

The following note on "safe arrival" cards is extracted from http://www.machinecancel.org/forum/hoboken_more/hoboken_more.html

A plan was devised to have 'safe-arrival' cards prepared in advance, and they would be mailed AFTER the transport arrived in France. Their processing was slow, and they were crowding the room. So he had a man connected with the firm which supplied canceling machines to the postal service to come and we worked out a design for a postmark. This postmark which showed a spread eagle and the words "Military Post Office Soldier's Mail" in two lines above, was approved by the General. With the electric canceller in use we could postmark the thousands of cards in a twentieth of the time it took by hand. Then . . . in spare time . . . sort them by states, cities, etc. and they were marked and stored until the cablegram came in stating that the ship had arrived. Half an hour later they were at Hoboken Post Office and on the way, so a wife in Chicago (for instance) would know next day of the loved one's arrival, instead of two weeks.

Roy's undated card read:

I have arrived safely. Roy

After the word "safely" is the word "OVERSEAS" inserted with a rubber stamp.

This is the front of Roy's "safe arrival" card.

POSTMARKED: U.S. ARMY POSTAL SERVICE
MARCH 2, 1918
IN FRANCE '18

Dear Home Folks:

I'm safe in port but still on the boat. Got in yesterday. We had a fine trip; I wasn't sick at all. We had splendid weather the last few days; warm clear days and moonlight nights. Nothing exciting occurred during the whole trip.

We had a prodigous feed Washington's Birthday. Roast turkey, pie, etc. I'll send the menu if I have time to copy it.

We're near a town, but I haven't had a chance to see anything much but the waterfront. Had a little glimpse of the narrow streets and the high steep roofs. The only thing I've seen that looked natural was a Ford. It was true to life. I can probably tell you a good deal more about it (The country, I mean, not the Ford) when I write again. Here is the menu I spoke of:

U.S.S. _____ *
Washington's Birthday, 1918

Menu
Celery Sweet Pickles
Cream of Celery Soup, Croutons
Roast Turkey
Giblet Gravy   Sage Dressing   Cranberry Jam
Mashed Potatoes   Sliced Beef Tongue
Combination Salad   Mayonnaise Dressing
Apples   Oranges   Raisins
Pie   Cake
Coffee
Cigars   Cigarettes

Will write you in a few days.

— Roy

This letter has illegible signature of a censor plus: O.K

We now know that the name of the ship was the U.S.S. President Lincoln and that this banquet took place in the harbor at St. Nazaire, France.

MARCH 12, '18

Dear Everybody at home,

Got a few of your letters and will try to answer them. Twenty-two of my long-lost have caught me lately; dates varying from Dec 14 to Feb 15. I was sure glad to get them. Got one from Uncle Robert, one from Jess, one from Clara, two from Mamie, one from Floyd, and whole stack of Mother's. R.W. said that Ben was in England.

You remember me telling you about writing to the boys at Kelly about my mail. One of them wrote me, enclosing a letter of Maude's, which was all he found. He went thru the offices, both at camp an in town, but found no packages. He said his folks sent him five but he didn't get any. Several of the boys have rec'd packages since getting here. The fellow that wrote me was one of the Whitman Co. boys who went to Texas with me. He said two of the fellows who went there are back at Vancouver cutting spruce. I've never heard from Joe, but saw some Spokane boys over here the other day. They were infantry from Camp Lewis.

I was as much surprised as you could have been to learn that you rec'd $28.50. Was it for Nov. and Dec., or Jan.? About Jan 1

I made out an allotment of $15. I'm sure I wrote you about it. The allotment was voluntary and was to take effect Jan. 1, the same as my insurance. The gov't adds nothing to voluntary allotments, so you should have rec'd $15 for Jan or $30 for Jan and Feb, but I can't understand the $28.50.

If allotments had taken effect when I came into the army that amt. would be just right for Nov and Dec, but I rec'd full pay for those months. The company records show the allotment as I wanted it. Perhaps when I get paid I can dope it out, but I can't see thru it yet.

The last week has been as pretty spring weather as I ever saw; warm clear days without a breath of wind.

We are in quarantine at present. It's about the same as it was at Hancock; the mail and laundry go and come as usual, and we drill and exercise. We simply can't run around as we please.

I'm under the best drill master I've had yet. We have a new captain and he's sure going to have us looking like soldiers. Drilling is fun when you can see it's getting you somewhere, but it's bum dope otherwise.

I'm getting sleepy, will finish later…

Next morning – another fine day. I can't add much to what I've written. I'm feeling fine –getting plenty to eat and nothing to do. I'll be glad when we get to work.

Well, Dad and Dorma here's hoping you had a good time your birthday and I wish I could have remembered you materially but couldn't be done. But we'll celebrate right next year.

I haven't seen any of the country yet, but will tell you something of it when I can. It is almost level here, only a little rolling. Very pretty country and every foot producing something. Hope you're getting along as well as I am. Lots of Love,

— Roy

March 23, '18

Dear Mother and Dad:

I intended to write yesterday, but didn't have time. Got two letters last night and will answer both at one shot. I'm still feeling fine and still getting fat. I'm afraid Uncle Sam will have to give me another uniform pretty soon or else put me to work.

I celebrated my birthday by helping clean up the "Y", laundering a little, and doing a little stunt or two with a pick and shovel. Didn't have time to write at all. Just got thru writing to Mamie. When you put Mamie's and this one together they may make something like a letter.

You said my last letter was dated three weeks before you wrote, so it was time then, or in a couple of days, for you to get the letter I left in New York. I suppose that by this time you have the letter I wrote and mailed at sea. The letters I got from you yesterday were written 2/11 and 2/28. In the same mail I got some books mailed in Scranton, Pa. Jan 28. You see it makes fine time. 22 days is very good, I think. I think you should get all my letters in from 3 to 4 weeks.

Since you got your $15 for January, it is evident that there is a mistake in the books. That $28.50 was paid to you but never charged to me. At least it hadn't been charged when I was paid last. I think the mistake will be found and the amount deducted from my pay: if not I'll straighten it up later.

It won't matter if they do cut my pay down that much, for I will have 3 months coming in about a week.

It's too bad there is such an unprecedented demand for my pictures. If I'd suspected it was to be, I'd have had a thousand of those pictures made. But I wouldn't advise you to have any made from those, or to get more from N.Y. either. If you want more tell me about how many and I'll get them over here. I think that would

Envelope, Censored Letter

be the best idea. Those pictures didn't suit me very well. The full length has a button unfastened, which is a high crime in the army, and the other is dim (?). So if you want more, let me have them made right.

It seems I've run out of anything to say, so guess I'd better quit.

— Love to everybody,

— Roy
Signed: O.K.
N. W. Jarrett
Lt. S.R.C.

YMCA LOGO
ON ACTIVE SERVICE WITH THE
AMERICAN EXPEDITIONARY FORCE
MARCH 28. 1918

Dear Home Folks,

Just a line to let you know I'm still thriving. Intended to write yesterday, but didn't have time, and have only a little time now.

This town is the most beautiful place I was ever in, I think, besides being full of historic buildings. *[Roy's diary was blank for this date, but it was probably either Blois or Abainville.]* I was out a little while last night looking around. There is a cathedral here, built in 1374, and another fine one used by several old kings of France. This building is several hundred years old. So, as I don't expect to be here more than a very few days at most, I'm making the most of my opportunity by going to see the sights every chance I have.

I'll write again in a day or two and tell you something of the country around here, and my trip on the train. That trip I'll never forget, for several reasons.

I'm feeling fine; think the hikes I'm getting will soon sweat some of the fat off. More news next time.

— Roy

Yesterday morning we set up our kitchen in the street in front of our quarters, and men, women and kids stood around and watched the proceedings. There's been from half a dozen to forty watching the cooks ever since. There have been only a few American soldiers here before, and we're still somewhat of a novelty to the inhabitants of the burg.

APRIL 5, 1918

Dear Everybody,

Again, I'm in a new camp, this time a French village, and so far as soldiers are concerned our company owns the town. Got in here day before yesterday, but have been so busy I haven't had time to write. The last letter I wrote used up my spare time (while

I was where I could write) for a week.

I think I told you there was a palace, or as the French call it, a chateau, in the town where I was last. Our Lieut. took the company thru one day last week. Our guide was a woman who talked the worst imitation of Americaine I ever heard, but we could see all right, even if we couldn't get the story connected with it. It was a great trip and I'll tell you more about it when I can. I simply can't describe the thing. I have some views of it, but can't mail them now.

I told you I would tell you something of my trip on the train, so here goes: The coaches (called wagons in French) are only about half the length of our cars, some of them less than that, and they have only four wheels each instead of eight or twelve. They are cross-partioned, dividing them into compartments. Most of them have five compartments, some more, some less. In each compartment are two seats facing together, and extending across the car crosswise from wall to wall. A door opens into each end of each compartment. Each comp. holds eight or ten people. Get the idea? They use a chain, hook and turnbuckle arrangement to couple the cars together, and prevent slack in the rig by spring bumpers. No automatic couplings and very few air-brakes. Tracks and engines seem generally good and capable of making good time,

The country where we are stationed now reminds me of the Palouse country more than anything I have seen. The hills occupy about as much territory, but are not so steep or so high as those at home, and there is an occasional clump of pines. Otherwise it reminds me very much of home.

I got some mail last night, all old stuff. There is some more to-day, so I won't send this until I see what it is. There might be something to answer.

This is a fine warm day. It has been raining most of the time for a week.

Didn't get any mail, so will send this along. Did you ever hear what happened to Clyde Myers? I suppose he is gone to the army ere this. The clippings you sent located several of the boys I'd been wondering about. I think Clyde should have made a captains' commission.

— Censor....T.R. R.W.Jarrett. Lt SRC

DIARY

Sat April 13
Rain day. Worked with engineer in morning.

Sun 14
Nice day. Went to Fuller's funeral. Got paid in forenoon.

Mon 15
Engineering in morning. Pick and shovel afternoon.

APRIL 17, 1918

Dear Mother and Dad:

Well, I've been paid off since I last wrote. Drew three month's pay Sunday morning. It amounted to $78, or 454.50f. Not so bad, considering insurance and allotment, is it? We were paid in French

YMCA Postcard

money, and it sure made some roll. Another pay day is due in from two to three weeks, and I had some money loaned out, so I sent you $35.08 (200 francs) thru the Y.M.C.A. It probably won't come thru as quickly as a letter, but it may.

I don't see why you're piling my money in the bank when you'd just as well be using it. It's no good to me either way until I get back, and I'm certain you could use it to advantage, so you'd better spend it.

Got a letter from Kerr's not long ago, and was very glad to hear from them. I will not answer at present, however, as I imagine they hear or see everything I write, and there is nothing different to tell.

I am becoming very proficient in the operation of an "Irish Anchor" *[slang for a shovel],* one of which I have been operating with great success the last couple of days. While I can't say that I'm extremely fond of the job, still it is not bad at all, and maybe there will be a change soon. We are building a road at present; don't know how long we will be at it.

The Material for our barracks is here, and they will soon be up. Then we will be thru with billet for some time, probably for good. We have to build them as well as a shop and various other fixtures.

Mamie tells me you have been paying postage on my letters. If so, somebody is badly mistaken, for we are told that postage is free. We can't pay it, and you're not supposed to. We were given printed cards, telling us what and how to write, and they say postage is <u>free</u>. So somebody is wrong.

Mother, I was very glad to hear you had joined the Star.* I'm going to do so myself sometime.

There is a movie on here to-night. There was one last Saturday night, and several of the French women came in. It was a good American play, and I suppose it was the first time these women had ever seen a movie, and of course they had never seen the scenes pictured, so it was great dope to them. The way they laughed and talked was more amusing than the play. Can't think of anything more. Love to everybody,

— Roy

* *Eastern Star, part of the Masonic Lodge*

DIARY

Sunday April 21
Plane came down near camp.
Inspected it.

Wed. 24
Working on railroad. Went to
Houdlincourt.

APRIL 25, 1918

Dear Everybody,

Everything is quite as usual. I'm feeling fine, working every day now. Still having rainy weather, but it hasn't rained any to-day. Yesterday it just poured nearly all day. It hinders our work a great deal for the soil we are working is partly sticky clay and the rest black loam, also sticky. Both are very difficult to handle when wet. The clay is about like the clay points at home, I think, only stickier. So you can imagine how we are getting along building roads and railroads by the hand powered method. We will get along twice as fast if it will ever quit raining. I used to think Camp Lewis was rainy, but it was a regular Sahara compared to this place.

Last Sunday a plane making a cross-country trip landed about half a mile from here with a broken gasoline line, and I had the pleasure of making a pretty thorough examination of it. It was very small, but was of the fastest type on the front (according to the aviator) being capable of 130 miles an hour. I couldn't swear to that, but I know she left the ground like she meant business. It was a French machine with an American aviator. I sure would like to have his job.

We were issued spiral leggings this evening (like the ones I wore when I had my picture taken). Hitherto we have been allowed to wear nothing but canvas.

Hope I get a letter soon. Haven't had any mail for over a week

Love to everybody,

— Roy
Censor signoff: O.K.
E.L.Hazard
1st Lt 2 Cav.

DIARY

Saturday April 27
Working on road. Issued spiral "puts"
[puttees]

Sun 28
Went to Houdlincourt and had a feed.
Rained all afternoon.

Mon 29
Worked on railroad. Signed payroll.

Tue 30
Mustered in. Worked on railroad. Throat
inspection. Bought a pen.

Wed May 1
Good day. Got up at 4:30 to unload rails
and structural steel.

Thur 2
Unloaded steel all day. Throat inspection
at night and moved to different barrack,
being a "diphtheria contact".

Fri 3
Digging well 12 ft square. Making
marvelous progress at it. First clear day in
months. Hot afternoon.

Sat 4
Hot cloudy day. Rain at night. Dug on

well. I am living in garage, but eating
with the bunch.

Sun 5
Raining nearly all day. Good breeze.
Nothing doing. Wrote some letters.

Mon 6
Worked on well. No excitement. Some
rain. Throat test.

Tue 7
Digging away still. Letters. Thunder
shower and hard rain after supper.

Wed 8
History repeats itself. Most of the boys got
out of quarantine.

Thur 9
Usual thing. Another throat culture; no
excitement.

Fri 10
Digging as usual. Hot cloudy day.

Sat 11
Everything as usual. Thunder shower in
evening. Throat culture. Paid after supper.

Sun 12
Mother's Day. Everybody had to write a
letter home before they could get a pass.
Cold rainy day. Nothing doing.

MAY 12, 1918

My Dear Mother:

This is Mother's Day, and the boys have been requested to write home to-day. This is my day to write, and I will make it a letter to you instead of to the whole family. Letters written to-day are supposed to go thru as special delivery stuff, so you should get this quicker than usual.

I just finished my dinner a little while ago. Had meat pie, spuds, bread, butter and rice pudding. Also ate half a can of sliced pineapple, so as Bertha says, "I feel quite full and nice."

You spoke about sending a nougat, but it isn't necessary. If the new ruling about parcels hadn't gone into effect, I'd say to send it along, but as it is, nothing doing. You see, we have to make out a request for whatever we want, and have it approved and signed by an officer. So I think that so long as shipping space is so valuable I can get along all right without it. We can get all the chocolate, oranges, figs, dates, etc., we want from the French and the Y, and we can get canned fruit, candy, jam, etc., at the commissary. So you needn't worry about me starving right away.

We got paid again last night. I drew the equivalent of $29.75, so it seems my pay is about $51.25. I don't know whether I'll send any of it home or not; don't think I will just now.

I understand we get a week's leave, plus necessary traveling time both ways, as soon as we have been here four months. Mine should come some time in July, and I want plenty of change on hand to last me thru. I'm going to England or Switzerland if I can, but don't think I can possibly get permission to leave France. There have been two or three camps established for men on leave, and that's probably where I'll spend it.

I'm still on the same old job, and probably will be for a few days, anyway, Weather the last week has been the same; showers and sultry, cloudy days. Tuesday night we had a big rain; about like the cloudburst we had at home a year or two ago. Had another thunder shower last night, and it's been raining intermittently to-day.

Have you heard how the winter was in Okanogan? I've been wondering if they had any more bad weather than you had.

Perhaps you think I should write oftener, but I have a lot of trouble filling a page a week. We just work eight hours a day, and one day is just like another. Don't move around or see anything new, so there's nothing to write.

Be good to yourself, and don't worry about me. Lots of love to you and Dad and the rest.

— Roy.
Censor signoff: O.K.
H.W.Jarrett

DIARY

Mon May 13
Cool breezy day. Everything as usual.

Tue 14
Ditto. Cold night.

Wed 15
Cold foggy morning. Hot and sultry
afternoon. Lots of artillery practice.

Thur 16
Another hot day. Lots of artillery practice
and sham battle at night.

Fri 17
Hot sultry day. Issued slicker suits and
boots.

Sat 18
another hot and sultry day. Thunder
shower in evening.

Sun 19
Another sultry day. Masonic meeting in
town but couldn't get to go.

Mon 20
Digging as usual. Hot day. Got out of
quarantine.

Tue 21
Hot day. Pick and shovel with gang.
Lecture at Y.

May 17, 1918

Dear Sis Dorma:

Well, how are you? I'm feeling as good as I ever did in my life, but I'm not quite as fat as I was last winter, or else my belt has stretched. I don't know which.

I've been getting letters from you kids occasionally, and decided I'd write to one of you to-night. I couldn't decide which one to write to first, so I counted your letters. You had two, and the other kids one apiece, so you get the first of the series, and the one with the next highest score when I get ready to write again will get the next one. How's that?

I was going to write last night, but waited until the mail came (about 7) to see if I'd get a letter from any of you. I didn't get any, and in the meantime I learned there was going to be a sham battle.

A class was graduating from the artillery school, and they pulled off a graduation stunt. So all our gang went over and about 10 P.M. when things were good and dark, the fun started.

One bunch stayed in a trench, and another bunch raided it. First thing they did was to explode a mine under the wire entanglements and blow them up. Then they charged. The guys in the trench kept things lit up like day with sky rockets and flares and other fire works, but it soon got so smoky from the rifle fire and fireworks that you couldn't see a man thirty yards away. And all the time the artillery was blazing away over their heads, the shells striking about half a mile behind, to keep imaginary reinforcements from coming up.

I wish you kids could have seen it, you would have enjoyed it immensely. It didn't interest us like it would have you because we'd seen about all that stuff before. The artillery school puts dozens of shells over our heads nearly every day.

We haven't had any rain for five days. Sunday was the last. M[onday] and T[uesday] were cool and breezy, fine days to work, but the last three have been scorchers, especially to-day. Received a slicker suit, slicker hat and hip boots to-night, so I don't suppose it will rain again for six months.

I suppose school will be out in about a week. What are you going to do then? And when are the folks going to Colville?

I got a letter from Ben last night. He's still cooking.

Well, I must quit. Write again soon. Lots of love,

— Roy

TUESDAY
MAY 21, 1918

Dear Everybody:

Will try and write a few lines before the lecture begins. Some kind of a talk at the Y. I think concerning the history of France.

The last week has been good weather; pretty hot, and we nearly melt after so much cold. But it seems good to have the sun shine a little—have had enough of rain and fog for present.

The work is going on quite as usual, except that one gang works in two shifts, so work goes on continuously from 5 A.M. to 9 P.M. The appearance of our camp has certainly changed during the last month, and will continue to change for a few months to come, I imagine.

There was a Lodge meeting in town last Sunday, but I didn't get to go because of the quarantine. I'm out now, and expect to go next Sunday if I don't have to work. Part of the gang work Sunday, and get Monday or Tuesday off. Several of the boys went over Sunday and I was sure peevish that I couldn't, but that didn't help a bit.

The Engineer in charge here made us a speech to-night about the work. Called us the "pets of the nation" and said "You fellows are in no more danger here than you'd be if you were herding goats on your Dad's farm, back in Texas." Now, does that make you feel any better? I've told you before we were not in any particular danger, but I don't know whether you'd believe me or not. *[Diary entry shows this was Abainville, France.]*

Mamie sent me some of the pictures of the gang taken down on the farm. They were good, and everything looked quite natural. I would give untold francs for a good Kodak here, and the skill to use it successfully. I could get some good stuff.

Well, this seems to be all I know, therefore <u>Finis</u>.

Love to all of you,

— Roy

DIARY

Wed May 22
Shoveling and unloading freight.
Mashed my thumb somewhat unloading
rails. Another day.

Thur 23
Hot cloudy day; thunder shower about
suppertime. Unloaded freight.

Fri 24
Breezy and cool. Fine day. Hauling sand
and gravel.

Sat 25
Went on 5 A.M. detail. Painting and
handling sash. Went to Gondrecourt.

MAY 25, 1918

Dear Sis Vella:

This is Saturday night, and I'm going to write you to-night, for I may have to work to-morrow, and I want to go to town to-morrow afternoon if I can. I have quit work on the big well I told you about. I am working with the crew now. Monday I dug on the well; Tuesday I ran a shovel and a "French Ford" (wheelbarrow); Wednesday shoveled dirt and unloaded steel off the cars; Thurs. unloaded hay, oats, bran and gravel; yesterday I hauled sand (on a narrow railroad) and unloaded heavy timbers and narrow guage car trucks, and to-day I ran a paint brush a while, then put up window sash. So you see I am still a Jack-of-all-trades.

Work is going along pretty lively now. We work in two shifts on the buildings. I am on the first shift. We get up at 4, go to work at 5; quit at 9; back at 1 P.M., quit at 5. That is the way it has been, but next week we get the other shift, and we'll have to work late.

I went down to the commissary this morning and bought me some candy and canned fruit and such dope. Between the Y and the canteen we get lots of such stuff. If you could look into my "trunk" now you would find chocolates, canned peaches, milk, pork and beans, salmon, chicken soup, cookies, gum, almonds and possibly a few oranges. How would you like to dig into that?

There is a lodge meeting in town to-morrow *[Abainville],* and if I have to work I'll sure be mad. A lot of good that will do tho.

Have you seen any pictures of soldiers with the new style "overseas" caps? We have them now, don't wear hats any more. I may have my picture taken that way so you can see how we look now. I'm glad they didn't have any more of those N.Y. pictures made, for I didn't like them. I'll get some more when I have a chance, but don't be impatient; I may not have a chance soon. Also, I'll find out how much I weigh when I can. I'm not as fat as I was.

Hope you kids are over the measles by this time. Have them right this time, so when you get into the army you won't be bothered with them.

Guess it's time to quit. Write often, and tell the other kids to do the same. I'm always glad to hear from you.

— Roy

Roy's handwritten copy of his will

Among the Roy's collection of books was a little 1917 volume titled, "Freehand and Perspective Drawing". Roy had written his name and A.E.F. address in the front. In the back, covering two blank pages is a handwritten copy of his will. The assumption that it is a copy is based on the fact that the two witness signatures are both in Roy's handwriting.

DIARY

Sun May 26
Nice warm day. Went to Houdlincourt,
Gondrecourt, and H. again. Meeting in
E.A. and M.M. degrees. 164th Infantry Sea
and Field Lodge. (N.D.)

Mon 27
Hanging sash with the crew. Cool and
breezy.

Tue 28
Cool and breezy. Hanging sash and
unloading cars. Got thru 11 P.M.

Wed 29
Usual weather and usual job.

Thur 30
Decoration Day. Warm. Went to
Houdlincourt. Athletic stunts. Sent
Mamie the papers.

Fri 31
Back on the same old job. No excitement.
Working on late shift this week. (8:22 to
12:45; 5:10 to 9:30)

Sat June 1
General work carpentering, hanging sash
and hauling steel.

Sun 2
Warm still day. Went to M.M.Lodge in
Gondre. Conferred 3rd Deg. on candidate
from Aberdeen. Went to H. after supper.
Crew changed to early shift.

Mon 3
Nice cool day. Got up at 3. Hanging sash
as usual. No excitement.

Tue 4
The same. Went to commissary during
rest period.

Wed 5
Went on ten hour shift. 7 to 12 - 1 to
6. Putting crane track in. Nice cool
weather.

Thur 6
The same. Trying to line up the crane
track, with indifferent results.

Fri 7
Same job but got done with it. Weather a
little warmer.

Sat 8
Putting up track in boiler shop and
lining up the A-beams thereof. Warmer
day. Feeling bum.

Sun 9
Hot day. Intended going to lodge but

nothing doing. Went to H. with Griner and
Swezey.

Mon 10
Working as usual. Got traveling orders at
noon and packed up same evening. Rain
night before and cloudy today.

Tue 11
Cloudy and threatening rain. On the
road to Langres. Arrived shortly after
noon. Swezey and I went to town at
night.

Wed 12
Went to work at 7 A.M. overhauling
Studebaker. Quit at 10 P.M.

Thur 13
Working ten hours on the same job.

Fri 14
The same. Helper sick and working alone.

Sat 15
The same

JUNE 13, '18
[LANGRES, FRANCE]

Dear Everybody:

Just a line to let you know that everything is all right. Have intended writing every day for nearly a week, but something has always prevented. It is only about five minutes before time to go to work.

I have moved since I wrote you. Have a new camp and a new job and I'm working to beat the Dutch. Last night we worked until 10 P.M.

The present job is better than the old, to my notion at least. I imagine if C.C.J.* could see me, he'd say I looked quite natural.

Don't know when I can mail this, as there are no mail arrangements yet. I'll write you again as soon as I have time.

— Roy
Censor: O.K.
H. W. Jarrett
Lt. S.R.C.

* C.C.J. is his friend, C.C. Johnson who had operated an auto repair shop in Colfax, and for whom Roy worked before entering the army. C.C. later joined the faculty at Washington State College where he taught drafting and some basic engineering courses which I took from him about 1950-51.

Return address on this letter's envelope:

— Sergt. R.E.Thompson
Co. 13 – 1ˢᵗ M.M. Regt. S.C.
Air Service, Am.E.F.

DIARY

Sun 16 June
Worked until noon. Went to Langres
afternoon.

Mon 17
Cool showery weather. Working on
Studebaker as usual.

Tue 18
Still showery. Camp is beginning to get
muddy. Finished Studebaker at noon
and started in on National 12. Lecture at
Y on French history.

Wed 19
Tearing down motor and grinding
valves. Still raining. Plane came down
near our barracks.

Thur 20
Still it rains. Usual work. Went to town
with Steve and got our supper.

Fri 21
Still raining. Camp is getting muddy
and boots are appearing. No excitement
except rumors of travel.

Sat 22
Everything as usual. Nothing of interest
to report.

Sun 23
Stahl and I went to reservoir forenoon.
Went uptown afternoon and had supper
there. 12th Co. left camp. No rain.

Mon 24
Better weather. Nothing unusual
otherwise.

Tue 25
Second lecture of series on French history
at Y. Empire of Charlemagne.

Wed 26
Finished motor and disassembled rear
axle. Got first mail since we reached this
camp.

Thur 27
More mail today. Warm day. Working
alone.

Fri 28
Nothing exciting. Went uptown after
work. Shop work getting rather slack.

Sat 29
Got my National done and worked on
Dodge. A.M. mechanics cause fire.

Sun 30
Close, Eckhardt and I went to cave of
Sebanus and the source of the Marne.
Came back somewhat weary. Signed

payroll and had inspection of barracks
bags. Warm day.

Mon July 1
Cloudy and cooler, but nothing new
except reveille. Working on a Dodge
sedan.

Tue 2
Nothing new. Cool weather

Wed 3
The same.

Thur 4
Stall, Trevathan, Wisdom and myself
visited cave and fort. Had a feed and
general good time. Took a lot of pictures.
Cool cloudy day.

Fri 5
Warmer weather. Working on Dodge sedan.

Sat 6
Nothing new. Finished my Dodge and
started in again on clutch.

Sun 7
Still hot day. Laundered. Went to lake
for swim in afternoon with Ross Dorland
and Basserman.

Mon 8
Another hot day.

Tue 9
Breeze and shower last night and cooler
today. Transfer to Ford Dept.

Wed 10
Another cool day. Went to town.

Thur 11
Fine lecture at "Y" on "My 2 years in
Germany" by Y man.

Fri 12
Warmer weather. Thing getting quieter
in Ford and passenger departments but
not in trucks.

Sat 13
Very quiet day in shop. Had fine concert
at new Y. Doughnuts and chocolate and
a swell time generally.

Sun 14
Warm day. Wrote letters and went up
town after dinner. Had my picture taken
and supper in town.

JULY 14, 1918

Dear Home Folks:

Sunday morning again, and nothing doing. This is Bastile Day and a holiday, but as we don't work on Sunday anyway, we are wishing it had been some other day so we would get two days off instead of one. It is cool this morning, and raining a little, but not enough to do us any good or any harm, except that it's good filling weather for the wheat.

We dedicated the new Y building last night. Not exactly dedicated, either, for there is to be formal dedication later, but the place was opened with a concert and treats (chocolate and doughnuts) for the boys. And to-day the place is full of fellows writing letters. Had a dandy time last night. A Frenchman and two French girls sang and played for us. They were fine. One girl sang in both Anglaise and Francais. She sang "Over There" and you should have heard the boys join in on the chorus. I'll bet they heard us five miles away.

A big lieutenant – I can't remember his name – put the building up. He is about as tall as Hugh C. and as wide as Jim C. One of the Y men made a talk, and thanked "Lieut. – and his gang of stevedores" for their good work, and called him up on the stage. The Lieut. came up and stood there while the Y man explained how difficult it was to obtain for him a present which would properly express their appreciation, etc., and after about ten minutes of this, Mr. Y. gave him a big 19¢ pocket knife with a long chain. You should have heard the boys yell. Then the Lieut. tried to make a speech, and the boys would cheer every sentence he got out of his mouth, so he said about fifteen words in about fifteen minutes. I think we enjoyed it more than he did.

I ordered some papers sent to you. I don't suppose you have ever got hold of "The Stars and Stripes", so I thot I'd send you a few. It has lots of funny stuff in it, and I imagine you will find it quite interesting.

Also have some clippings here which I will send if I can find them. Usually, I can't find anything I want when I want it. Don't know how it will be this time.

I haven't had my picture taken yet, but may have it to-day. I am going up town this afternoon and will see about it.

Tell Lou not to worry about that coat, for it will probably be out of style before I need it, anyway. Its too bad you didn't find anything in Okanogan, but you probably will fare better this fall. Did you go see Miss Kenny? She had the place up on the hill near Wiley's. I saw her in Omak.

What has been done about the highway up Goose Flat to Omak and Okanogan? Nothing, I suppose, under the conditions. Did Ted get anything before he enlisted?

Well, I am out of anything to write, so must quit.

Love to everybody.

— Roy

Monday 15th – Went up town yesterday and had some pictures taken, but can't get them for a week yet.

DIARY

Mon 15 July
Hot day. Not very busy. Lots of fellows went to lake for a swim.

Tue 16
Another hot day. Shop rather quiet.

Wed 17
Another scorcher. Business improving. Moved back to passenger dept. Cleaned up the camp for some generals approval.

Thur 18
Fierce wind and rain storm last night. Much cooler.

Fri 19
Warmer again but not so hot as Wed.

Sat 20
*Pretty hot day. Sending out lots of truck
trains.*

Sun 21
*Cool cloudy day. Nixon and I hiked thru
tunnel, visited fort and cave. Covered
about 16 miles. Supper in town.*

JULY 21, 1918

Dear Everybody,

Will try to write a little tonight. I have been hiking around all day. Started out about 10:30 and went thru the canal tunnel. It is 3 miles long, and sure some tunnel, about 35 feet wide, I guess. It is walled clear thru with hand-cut stone blocks, and believe me, they used several. When we got into the tunnel a couple of hundred yards we could see the other entrance, but for a long time we thot it was a light on a canal boat, it looked so small. The echoes in there are great; yell, and it echoes for five minutes. Well, we walked through the tunnel and about a mile further down the canal, took to the hills and covered another mile or two, when we found a signpost reading "_____ 12.7 Km". *[Roy left this blank to save the censor some effort.]* Or just about 8 miles. We tried to get some chow, but nothing doing, so we beat it for town, got our supper, and then to camp. Covered all together about 16 miles, but it was worth it.

Had some pretty hot weather lately. Thursday night (I think it

Tunnel, Meholle Canal de la Meuse, Near Houdlincourt, France
as it appeared in June 2006

was) we had a prodigious breeze which collapsed some barrack buildings and leveled a few tents. Our barrack stood up all right, only some of the roofing blew off, and thereafter the roof leaked more or less.

I was surprised to hear of Mr. Newell's death, as I hadn't even heard of his sickness. Also Vera Sorrels and the Kinger baby. It was too bad. I had never heard before about Kinger's being there.

Now, in regard to the camera: All you'll have to do is write the War Dept and get the orders changed so that we will be allowed to keep a camera. Then I'll send the order for it. Until then, nothin' doin'. However, I appreciate your kindness very much, and some day soon I'll send an order for some articles of chow.

I got my pictures to-day, but they're horrible. I'm sending one and think I'll burn the rest. They don't suit me a-tall. They may suit me better when I get a good look at them in daylight, which I haven't had yet. But I think I'll ditch them.

It's getting late and I'm <u>slightly</u> tired, so must quit and roll in. Hope to get some letters soon. I should have about a dozen I've never got.

— Roy

It's too bad about C.C.J, but it is really no more than I expected, knowing what I did of his business methods. That wasn't the job he was cut out for.

[This is the same C.C. Johnson referred to in the letter of June 13, 1918]

DIARY

Mon 22
Worked forenoon. Sick afternoon.

Tue 23
Cool and rainy. Went on sick call, marked "Duty", excused at shop and went back to bed. Bed all day.

Wed 24
Working again. Feeling pretty good. Barrack drill after supper.

Thur 25
Showery weather. Nothing much doing.

Fri 26
The same. Feeling fair, but not so good as usual.

*World War I Auto Mechanics crew at Camp Holabird, Maryland
Photo taken by Henry Williams (standing second from right in group
of four). Photo donated by Neil Rozman, Strongsville, Ohio, great-
nephew of photographer. No known photo of Roy's group exists.*

FRIDAY, JULY 26, 1918

Dear Everybody:

Am going to try to write, but there is so much noise in circu-
lation I doubt if I have much luck. It is about 9:15, I guess (my
watch is on the bum, as usual) and everybody is going to bed and
yelling and laughing so it sounds like a chivarri. These motor mechanics are the craziest guys on earth.

I have been laundering a little to-night. Don't do much of that
any more, but things were pretty handy to-night so thot I would
wash a little.

I felt rather bum the first of the week. Laid off work a day and
a half, but wasn't very sick. Am all right again now. The first day
I have missed for three or four months.

Weather has been cloudy and cool the last week. Have had

several showers.

This job is hopeless *[letter writing]*. The air is full of Ameri-caine, French (?), Spanish, Italian, Greek and a few more. We'll finish to-morrow.

Sat. morn ---- Had a good rain last night, and prospects for more. Wish you had it if you still need it as badly as you did.

Had a letter from Mamie last night, and one of Clara the night before, and one from you each time. Mamie sent a couple of little pictures. They are certainly fine.

It is just about time to go to work, and as I want to get this out this morning, I'll have to quit. More next time.

— Roy

The American drive this week is creating lots of excitement. Suppose it is there, too.

DIARY

Sat 27
Fine concert at the Y by two American girls.

Sun 28
Inspection, personal and medical.
Personal cancelled after we were ready.
Went to town, rode on geared road
and attended Masonic club. (its first
meeting). Supper in town.

LANGRES. — La Crémaillère au Pont. — The cable-railway.

Geared Railway, Langres

Mon 29
Better weather. Checked up and
packed our bags, ready to move. Met
a guy from 91st Div. First I had heard
that they were over.

Tue 30
Got up at 4:30 and boarded the
train. Stopped from 11:30 'til 6 at
Neufchateau. Got into Gondrecourt at
8 and rode to camp in trucks.

Wed 31
Hot day. Lay around all morning.
Put sheet iron on powerhouse after
noon.

July 31, 1918

Dear Mother and Dad:

Well, I'm back at my old camp *[Gondrecourt]* and my old job. What do you know about that? We left the other one *[Langres]* yesterday morning and got in here last night. We moved by train this time, and rode first-class at that. We generally ride third. I can't understand how it happened, but we didn't kick any. This is the same old place. Very little has been done since we left, and we are starting work just where we quit seven weeks ago. Got in at 8:30 last night, and went to work at noon.

Thirty of the boys get a week's vacation soon. The clerk read their names out to-night. They go in the order of enlistment. This bunch came in Sept 5 to 20. I'll probably get mine about January. Wish I could get it now, during the hot weather, but don't think it can possibly come before Sept. and probably later than that. But I'll sure take it when it comes, if the snow is thirty feet deep. If I can't go swimming I'll get me some skis and bust my knee again.

I'm going to start in to-morrow night on a series of French lessons which come three a week. And one of the boys offered to help me with my algebra and furnish a book. I'm going to be crowded for time, but both chances are too good to miss so I'll have to find time some way.

The big Y we were putting up before we left is working now. Big show on to-night. And the Salvation Army has a building here now, so we can get pie, doughnuts, etc. They don't sell tobacco but they sell candy which suits me just as well, and is a lot harder to get.

This seems to be all I know, and I am horribly tired to-night. Love to all of you,

— Roy

DIARY

Thur Aug 1
Horribly hot. Putting on roofing and the heat was fierce. Took first French lesson.

Fri 2
Cool and showery. Putting on roofing. Got rained out at 4:45, after several smaller showers. Beaucoup mail.

Sat 3
Roofed until 10, then hauled cement in O.W.D. until 5 P.M. Showery. More mail.

Sun 4
Cloudy and cool. Cutting roof lumber all day.

Mon 5
Cloudy and showery. Putting on roofing. Got our traveling orders.

Tue 6
Packed up. Waited till 9 o'clock for definite orders. Dinner at 11, got on box cars at 2:30. Stopped at Neufchateau 2 hrs. Got into Langres at 11:30 and to camp at 1 A.M. Showery.

Wed 7
Shifting around, building bunks, and getting settled down generally. No work. Cloudy and cool.

A.P.O. 714
AUGUST 7, '18

Dear Mother and Dad:

As you will perhaps notice by the above, I have moved again. *[back to Langres]* We left 703 June 11 and came here. (714) Stayed until July 30, then moved back to 703. Stayed there until yesterday morning, and moved here again. Left there yesterday about 2:30, traveling in side-door Pullmans *[army slang for "box-cars"]*. Got in this morning at 1 A.M. I will confess that I can't see the reason for it all. I wish we could go to a new place every move, it's no fun this way.

We were working pretty hard while at our old railroad camp. Some of the boys wanted to stay there, and some wanted to come back here. Personally, I didn't want to do either; preferred a new camp altogether, but I've noticed that my wishes are not regarded as much as they should be.

Got the pictures all O.K. a couple of days ago. They are good of you, I think. Everything looks natural except Dad's lip and the service pins. I didn't know before that you were wearing those, (the pins, I mean) And I didn't know Dad had removed the mustache again. I'm due for a service bar tomorrow. A gold V-stripe on the left sleeve, denoting six months with the American Expeditionary Forces.

We went on board ship Feb. 8. It seems more like six weeks.

The Americans have been doing great things up front of late, haven't they? Some of the boys think things will be settled this fall. I think it is rather early to judge yet, as the Americans have only lately got into things on a large scale. Also, a great deal depends on the Russian situation. What do you think about it? You hear more news than we do.

You said Harry would soon be home. Is he on leave or dis-

World War I "Blue Star" pin, worn in honor of a person in the
military. Size: 9/16" x 5/16" Star is Blue, surrounded by gold border
on white field. Stars around outside are red with gold border. Roy's
father and mother each wore one.

charged? And what was wrong with him?

I suppose you have seen pictures of the little narrow-gage trains and read descriptions of them. I examined some not long ago, and they are great rigs. Little flat cars, with the floor only about two feet from the ground. They are about twenty feet long. The locomotives of course interested me most. They are about the size of an ordinary 20 hp traction engine; weigh about 10 tons, I was told. The drivers are about 18 inches high; six of them. The gage of the track is 60 cm. (about 24 inches)

It's time to quit, I guess. More next time.

Yours Truly,
The Family Hero

DIARY

Thur 8
Went into shop at old job. Working on
Winton with Armstrong.

Fri 9
Another Winton job. No particular
excitement.

Sat 10
On a Dodge job. Ghost took his monthly
stroll at 7:30 with his usual 169 francs.

Sun 11
Went up town in the morn. Stayed till
after supper. Went to Masonic Club and
joined the same. Ice Cream at Y but
didn't manage to get any.

Mon 12
Nice day. Working on Benz (German).
Took in French lesson at Y but didn't
learn a great deal.

Tue 13
Warm day. Everything quiet in shop.

TUESDAY, AUG 13, '18

Dear Homefolks:

Just had dinner and have a few minutes before time to go to work again. It is a warm sunny day, with a slight breeze.

Everything here is going quite as usual. Don't know of any excitement at present.

Friday night service chevrons were issued to us; three each, for blouses and overcoat. Saturday night the ghost took his monthly stroll thru the camp, and as a result, some of the boys were a trifle hilarious Sunday. But I haven't heard of a single fight, so I guess all is well now. Haven't had any mail for a week, but expect some to-night. (Whistle blows: time to go to work.) 7:15 - Will try it again. No mail yet, but have hopes of getting it to-morrow.

I have been working the last couple of days on a German car. You may have heard of the Benz. It seems there is some difficulty in getting parts, as she is rigged out with parts from American, French and Italian cars. She is a grand old bus, tho, with lots of pep. Don't know whether she was captured, or came to France before the war. She's S.C. *[Signal Corps]* property now, anyway.

It certainly is some job to write letters from here. To-day is just like yesterday and to-morrow, and nothing to tell in any of them. Haven't got a letter lately, as there is nothing to answer..

Somebody gets stewed occasionally and starts something. One of the boys was up-town a few nights ago, and took on a few too many. Met some Q.M. *[quartermaster]* fellows in the same condition, and they told him how much better Q.M. men were than M.M. *[motor mechanics]*. He denied the statement rather emphatically, and they proceeded to work his face over with a quart bottle of champagne.

Peeled him up a little, but he's getting over it. The same night another guy from our bunch got in a dice game with a couple of

Engineers that he thot were drunker than they actually were. He raked in more than he had coming and thot they wouldn't notice it. They let it go a while, then one of them, a big six-footer, landed a right-hander on his lamp without saying a word. It was over two weeks ago, and that eye is still black. I wasn't sorry tho. The guy is no good; does nothing but beat the fellows out of their money, so I wouldn't have cared if they'd hit him on both sides and made them match. Guess you can see I have nothing to write.

—Roy

DIARY

Wed, Thur, Fri Aug 14, 15, 16
Hot sultry weather. Nothing much doing.
Still working on Benz.

Sat 17
Sent Benz out and began on Dodge in
horrible shape. No change in weather.

Sun 18
Hot and sultry. Inspection and gas mask
drill until 12:30. Got some mail at last.

Mon 19
Doing Dodge bearings and valves.
Weather hot.

Tue 20
Still on bearings. Some guy has tried to
stop main knock by taking up too much
on rods. Still hot.

Wed 21
Same job. Hottest day we have had.
Little mail came in. Lecture at Y.
"Womanhood" Finest I ever heard.

Thur 22
Hotter yet. Still on the Dodge.

Fri 23
And still hotter today. Thunder at night,
but very little rain. Hear that Toul drive
has started, but nothing definite.

Sat 24
Cooler and showery. Working on brakes,
which like everything else are in horrible
shape. Got a little mail.

A.P.O. 714
AUG 24 *[1918]*

Dear Homefolks:

Just a few lines to-night. I am still able to hit the chow line thrice daily and get away with most of the eatables that come my way.

We have had some fearfully hot weather the last week. Last night about dark it clouded up and gave us some thunder and lightning, and tried to rain. Didn't have much luck, but has done better to-day – several nice little showers, and much cooler.

Things have been pretty lively in the shop the last week. Enough work to keep everybody busy. I'm getting some valuable experience out of it, and I think all the others are, too, tho some of them have been in the business ten years or more. It is very different, in some ways, from common garage work. We get more total wrecks here for one thing. About half that come in are on their last legs. For instance, my partner and I (we work in pairs) have been working for a week on a Dodge that came in for salvage. They decided she was good enough to fix up, and we are doing our best. She was in horrible shape, due partly to ignorance and partly to natural causes. The number of collisions, especially among the trucks, is considerable. So they come in with sprung frames and smashed radiators and burned brakes and burned bearings. We work from the standpoint that the drivers know nothing as all, hence cars must be in the best possible shape before leaving. Lack of parts is a great trouble. It is obviously impossible to keep in stock parts for hundreds of cars, as storage and transportation conditions are at present. So it is up to us to fix the old parts or make new ones. As it is sometimes impossible to do either we sometimes borrow parts from other guy's cars. That is prohibited, but everybody does it. So if a car sets on the floor a few days there's not much left but the frame and body.

Don't know what you'll think of this mess I've written, but I almost live in the shop, and cars are all I know.

What did you do about the big ranch*, and what are you going to do? I'd tell you what I think of it, only you've never told me much about the thing.

Got a letter from Clara to-night, written July 20. I don't see why we don't get some mail. Practically none for three weeks. Will appreciate it so much more when it does come.

Love to all of you,

Roy

Glad you got that $35 finally. I'd begun to think you never would.

*Roy's parents looked for several years before finding a hay ranch at Colville, Washington, where they moved shortly after WWI, about 1920

Diary

Sun Aug 25
Worked forenoon. Went to club afternoon.
Bought a Luger. Went to work after supper
but nothing doing.

Mon 26
Went to work as usual. Transferred to
truck work. Cooler weather.

Tue 27
Moved after supper to new barrack. No
excitement otherwise.

Wed 28
Signed payroll - turned in bacon cans -
issued R.C. pajamas and sox.

Thur 29
Went on sick report and to see dentist. No
work.

Fri 30
No excitement.

Sat 31
Pay day. Drew our francs after retreat.
Quiet day otherwise.

SAT. AUG 31, '18

Dear Everybody:

Well, how are "you all" to-day? I am about as usual and still getting lazier daily, as you can see by my letters.

I have been working all week, except Thursday when I went to see the dentist. Will work tomorrow forenoon and get Monday forenoon off. Visit the dentist again Tuesday. It's the same old story – fillings.

Weather has been much better the last week – partly cloudy and cooler. Much better working, too. I have been working on trucks this week, but expect to go back to touring cars soon. Hope so, anyway. I don't like truck work as well, tho the experience is good.

Drew our pay to-night. We have never been paid so early before, generally get it between 4th and 15th.

Several of the boys left on their vacation the first of the week. They get a full week to play in and traveling time both ways. Pretty good isn't it? They all say they have a grand time. Wish I could get mine during the hot weather, but don't see any chance.

Haven't had any more pictures taken, but will when I have a chance to get any good ones.

This is not much of a letter, but it's all I can think of.

— Roy

DIARY

Sunday Sept 1
Warm quiet day. Worked forenoon,
laundered and wrote letters after.

Mon 2
Bunk fatigue forenoon - worked after.

Tue 3
Went to dentist. No work.

Wed 4
Moved back to passenger cars. Rush job
with Cad 8. Worked after supper.

Thur 5
Torrential showers began in night and
lasted all day. Worked all day and at
night. Trouble with brakes.

Fri 6
Still showery today. Finished Cad and
worked on Dodge and Winton. First
furlough bunch came back.

FRIDAY, SEPT 6. [1918]

Dear Mother and Dad:

Rec'd your letter three days ago but have been working every
night and haven't had time to answer. Been on a rush job* and
worked from 7 a.m. to 8 or 9 p.m. Got the old boar out today, so
am feeling better. *[Diary identifies this rush job as a Cad 8...trouble with the brakes. Old boar, must be referring to the Cad 8.]*

Have been getting lots of rain the last two days. Rains a while
and then the sun shines a while and then some more rain. And
when it rains, it rains, believe me.

[This "rush job" fits with the A.E.F. push at the front.]*

The boys that had a furlough got back to-night. They all say they had a fine time. Another bunch goes to-morrow or Sunday. I think I'll apply for one tomorrow. May get it the 16th. I want to go while the weather is still good. Don't know yet whether I'll go to Aix les Bains or Marseille. Can't decide between them. Ben wrote me he would go to Aix les Bains the fifteenth.

I can't locate your last letter just now, so don't know what questions you asked me. Will hunt it up and write some more in a day or two. Haven't time to write more now, and am horribly tired besides.

Love to all of you,

— Roy

DIARY

Sat 7
Dodge and Winton work. Afternoon off for night work earlier in the week. Went to new French class.

Sun 8
Wrote letters and went to club meeting.

Mon 9
Cold and rainy. Everybody wearing boots and the camp gets muddier every day.

Tue 10
Nothing to report

Wed 11
Showery and cold. No excitement.

Thur 12
Warmer and no rain.

Fri 13
Good weather. Working on Natl [ional]
(12).

Sat 14
No rain today. Went uptown to banquet
of Masonic Club. Nurses came in.

Sun 15
Patients came in. Hot sultry day. Work in
spare parts, opening cases.

SUNDAY EVENING SEPT 15 *[1918]*

Dear Everybody:

I hope you'll forgive me for not writing last week, but I didn't have an idle evening all week, and have worked all day to-day. I went up town last night and had a feed. Our club *[Masonic Lodge?]* had a banquet – about 150 present, I guess – and believe me, we had some time. We listened to some songs and speeches, and had some real live singing by the whole crowd. Just about the time we got going in good shape, the police made us clear out, owing to regulations about lights.

I got your letter 8/15 since I wrote, also one from Clara and two or three from Mamie.

I was somewhat surprised to hear Simpson's are coming back. What's the matter with Montana?

My pass is due a week from to-day, but I rather expect passes to be stopped for a while now, on account of the battle. Things are going fine on the front, aren't they?

We have had fine weather lately. No rain for about four days now. The mud is about gone. To-day has been simply perfect, warm and bright. The mornings are pretty cool since the big rain, so it takes a prodigous effort to get out of bed in the morning.

Mamie tells me she is going to spend a month or so at home and help out with the work. I think it is a good idea.

What was wrong with the wheat this year? I had heard that crops would be poor, but didn't suppose it would be as bad as it seems to be.

And tell me all about the new draft law. I have read a little, but don't know just how the law is or how classifications are made, or who had to register. I suppose just about all the men I know are registered now.

Got a letter from Bill Smith the other day. When he wrote the first part he was a street car conductor, and when he finished he had enlisted in the Med. Corps and was at Fort Lawton. Was in the hospital then with a touch of blood-poisoning, but expected to get out the next day.

Well, I must quit,

Love to everybody,

— Roy E. Thompson
Co 13, 1st M.M.Regt. S.C.
Air Service, A.E.F.

DIARY

Mon Sept 16
Warm weather. Usual work. Nat'l
bearings. Some job.

Tue 17
The same. Worked on spare parts from 7
to 10 P.M., missing my French lesson.

Wed 18
Cool and showery. Part of the shop crew
on S.P., but not me.

Thur 19
Nothing to report. Usual showery weather.

Fri 20
Rainless day and cold moonlight night.
Much the coldest we have had. Feeling
bum. Took laundry uptown.

Sat 21
Went to French class. Nurses and officers
had a dance. Had quite a chat with one
of the nurses. Clear and cold.

Sun 22
Beaucoup rain. Laundered and wrote
letters. Went up town after noon. No club
meeting.

Mon 23
Showery. Armstrong absent. Sent
Nat'l out for test. Didn't pass.
Went with stevedore gang at 4:30.

*Following letter was in the bundle. The light hand, faded ink,
and oxidized paper made it almost unreadable....But we figured
it out.*

SEPT. 29, 1918
MRS. G. A. THOMPSON
ALBION
WASHINGTON
U.S.A.

My dear Mrs. Thompson:

Of course you are wondering why you have a letter from me.
So I will tell you immediately it is because you have a splendid
son who is not forgetting Mother while he is doing his "bit".

Yesterday we went for a walk and on the way Roy walked
beside me for a while and as we talked I thought I saw a look in
his eyes which I decided to investigate.

To make a long story short what he wanted was to have some-
one write home to Mother that he is all right, because he knows
she is worrying and he doesn't like to think she is doing so.

Blessed boy I nearly hugged him right there.

He certainly looks fine and is one of our young <u>American
Princes</u>.

If you knew them as I do, just thousands of them, you would
say as I do, "Glory to God in the Highest". You cannot describe
them if you try.

I have no hesitation in assuring you your boy is all you would have him, a credit and a pledge of his Mother's upbringing.

I remain

Sincerely yours

— (Miss) Gertrude J. Ferre
Y.M.C.A. Canteen,
France

DIARY

Tuesday 24 Sept 1918
Langres, France
Passes came in. Quit early to pack up.

Wed 25
Langres to Dijon, France
Nice day. Med. Inspection. Red T. took us to train. Changed at Chalindry. Got into Dijon about 2 p.m. Inspected the city.

Thur 26
Dijon to Aix les Bains, France.
Got up quite early and caught 1:46 train. Aix [les Bains] at 7:a.m. Checked in, went to hotel and had breakfast. Went up Mt. Revard afternoon. Y. at night.

Fri 27
Aix les Bains
Got up at 10. Took trip on the lake and visited the abbey. Lawson and I had supper with two R.C. girls. Had fine time. Went to train and got them a seat.

SPECIAL ORDERS NO. 39 authorized Roy's leave at Aix les Bains. The original document is 5-1/2" x 8". The original is a carbon copy on flimsy, pocket-worn paper. This is the only official document found with Roy's letters that carries his serial number. It carries three rubber stamps. Two are on the back. The ring says "Assistant Provost Marshal No. 99 A.E.F." These two include a date stamp, but no signature. They include rubber-stamped dates "26 SEP 1918" and "4-OCT 1918". The stamp on the front reads the same in the outer ring except it shows "No. 89", and is dated and signed in the middle, "10-4-18 Lyon, M.M." The back of these orders also carries a rubber-stamped authorization:

Subsistance and quarters in kind furnished on this leave
in Savoie Leave Area
from 26 Sep 1918 to 4-Oct 1918.
R.J. Doughty
Captain, Quartermaster U.S.R.Q.M.

The bottom line on the front side, written in French, apparently grants travel at 1/4 of standard rate.

AMERICAN EXPEDITIONARY FORCES
ADVANCE SECTION   SERVICES OF SUPPLY
ADVANCE M.T. OVERHAUL PARK #1

23rd September, 1918.

SPECIAL ORDERS)
    NO.   39   )

Par. 1.   Under the provisions of Par. 3, G.O. #6,
G.H.Q., A.E.F., e.s., the following troops of Co. 13,
1st M.M.R.S.C., A.S., are granted a leave of absence
of seven (7) days, effective on 24th September, 1918
with permission to vist Aix les Bains (Savoie), France.

        Pvt. Boyd 267057 Joseph C.
        Sgt. Lichtenstein 266990 Lewis
        Cpl. Barry 267031 William E.
        Sgt. Buckley 266949 Thomas P.
        Cpl. Shapiro 267005 Joseph J.
        Sgt. Lohren 266958 William E.
        Sgt. Ryan 266996 James F.
        Cpl. Green 266984 Harold W.
        Cpl. Kring 267038 Raymond
        Sgt. Thompson 266969 Roy E.

    Accomodations in this leave area authorized by
telegram 1843, Sept. 21st, 1918, Deputy Provost Marshal
General.

    By direction of Lt. Col. BREWSTER-GREENE:

                    G. A. BOGGS,
                    2nd Lt. QMC USA
                    Adjutant

Armee Americaine Permissionaire Quart de Tarif.

Sat 28
Aix les Bains
Went to bed at 1 a.m. Up at 10. Afternoon
went to tennis court, bicycling, etc.
Dinner at Y. Had picture taken.

Sun 29
Aix les Bains
Not much excitement. Went bicycling all
afternoon with L. Baron and Boyd.

Mon 30
Aix les Bains
Rained all day. Dance at Y afternoon.
Went to show with Miss H. of 34 B.[ase]
H.[ospital] and to train afterwards.

Tue Oct 1
Aix les Bains
Went to Dent du Chat with Miss Buxton.
Rowed across Lake Bourget, climbed mt.
And return. Came back in one boat with
Frenchman. Splendid time. Dance at Y

Wed 2
Aix les Bains
Beaucoup weary. Rose at 11 a.m. Took a
few pictures. Went to Y. after supper.

Thur 3
Aix les Bains
Bummed around all day. "Stunt Night" at
Y. Took that in with Miss Fitch.

Fri 4
Lyons
Had packages censored Checked out at 1:30
and again at 5:30. Got into Lyon at 10.
Took in sights and went to bed.

Sat 5
Base Camp [Sampigny]
Left Lyon at 7. In Dijon from 1 to 3. Got
back to camp about 11 after riding the
slowest trains in France.

Sun 6
Cold day. Feeling rather bum. Nixon
and I took a hike afternoon.

Mon 7
Went to work at usual time. On Cad with
Barry. Spare Time Dept. after 9 o'clock

Tue 8
Spare time some more. Cold day. Feeling
dyspeptic and pepless. Went to French class.

OCT 8, 1918

Dear Homefolks:

Well, I'm back at work again. Left Aix *[les Bains]* Friday evening and got back to camp Saturday night about 11. Made pretty good train connections. Had good trains most of the way, but the last eight hours was on a train that would make the "Burgville

Special" freight look like a lightning express. It made about thirty miles in the eight hours.

That vacation was the most enjoyable eight days I have spent since I left home. Partly because I could do just <u>what</u> I wanted to when I wanted to – could stay in bed all day if I felt like it. Furthermore, there were real American women there. Lots of Y.M. and Red Cross girls spend their vacations in Aix. I talked with more American girls there every day than I had in the previous eleven months. Furthermore, real ice cream was to be obtained there, a <u>very</u> interesting feature. It cost two francs a dish, but it was worth a dollar.

I think I told you about all the trips I took, except one the last day I was there. It was a hike of three miles to some very beautiful gorges and waterfalls. Another very interesting thing was an old-style water power saw mill, located at the falls. It had one saw, of the bucksaw type, and turned out about a board an hour. Also, there was a small circular saw for edging.

I hope you get the pictures and other stuff I sent. I had the pictures taken there. I intended getting some good mounted ones, but learned that they couldn't produce that kind in less than eight days, and I wouldn't wait so long. I think they are pretty good, but I hope my legs are not normally as crooked as they look. We took a lot of pictures around there with a rented Kodak. Had very poor luck, tho. We couldn't get Eastman film and had to use French. They say only an expert can get good results with them.

This camp is rainy as ever. The last two days have been rainy and of course it is muddy. Only had one stormy day at Aix. I think the weather is better than here. I am sure it is warmer.

It is bedtime. Oh yes, I got two letters when I got back – written at Juliaetta and Lapwai. Wish I could have had some of that watermelon you had and didn't need.

Love to everybody.
           — Roy

Sgt. R. E. Thompson
Co 13, 1st Motor Mech. Regt. S.C.
A. S., American E.F. France

Photo of Roy standing, showing overseas service chevron and Aero Service Insignia on cap, is most likely the photo he refers to having taken at Aix les Bains while on leave. Stripes showing rank were only worn on the right sleeve in 1918.

DIARY

Wed 9
Clear but cold. Spare parts until 3
P.M., then back to work in shop, to our
considerable joy.

Thur 10
Coldest morning we have had. Beaucoup
frost. Usual work, letters and French class.

Fri 11
On Cad. Pulling motor, doctoring clutch
& trans. No particular excitement.

Sat 12
Cad. forenoon. Dodge after. Putting in
motor. French class.

Sun 13
Worked forenoon. Afternoon went to
Club meeting. While there we heard that
Germany had accepted the peace terms.
Rainy afternoon.

Mon 14
Worked all day and until 10 P.M. Getting
ready to move camp.

Tue 15
The same. Went back to the old Cad. at 3
P.M. Barracks were searched for tools and
park property.

Wed 16
Had inspection in forenoon. Checked
up on our wearing apparel. Worked
afternoon and night.

Thur 17
Worked all day and until 9:15. Packed
up tools and sent them out. Sent all cars
to Neufchateau.

Fri 18
Ordered to stay in barracks forenoon. No
move. Detail afternoon but very little to
do. Packed up.

Sat 19
Detail. Went for hike and uptown
afternoon.

Sun 20
Got up at usual time. Ready to leave at 8
o'clock, but didn't leave until 12:30. Left
Langres about 6 P.M. Stopped for night
about 11 o'clock.

Mon 21
On the road early. Got into Sampigny
about 2:30. Nice day. Saw antiaircraft
barrage about 7:30. Very interesting.

Tue 22
Cool and trying to rain. Put up stoves all
day.

Wed 23
Putting up stove foundations and leveling kitchen floors. Nice warm day. Boche tried to cross about 11:00, about 3, and twice about 7:30. Fine barrage and very interesting show generally. Lights prohibited.

Thur 24
On spare parts and lumber. Unloading cars and hauling junk around the park. Conglomerated mess gets in operation.

Fri 25
Cloudy weather and no air work. Stevedore work in yard.

Sat 26
The same. Went up town after supper. Nothing doing worth mentioning.

Sun 27
Worked forenoon. After went to trenches with Swezey and Blakening. Didn't get to see much, owing to lack of time. Clear cold night. Can hear big guns very plainly.

Mon 28
Working around yard on lumber and boxes. Fine clear day. Guns busiest they have been since we came here. Cold night.

Tue 29
Fine clear day. Working in yard. Lots
of planes over. Boche dropped a bunch
of propaganda, which we collected for
souvenirs.

Wed 30
Another fine clear day. Stevedore detail.
No excitement in particular.

Thur 31
Fair day. Several planes over. Lovely
barrage.

Fri, November 1
Cool and cloudy. Usual job.

Sat 2
Cold and cloudy. Rained all afternoon.
Lots of excitement about the Austrian
surrender.

Sun 3
Worked half day. Paid at noon. Went to
trenches in truck. Had only a little time
and didn't see much. Rained all night.

Mon 4
Cool and partly cloudy. Couple of Boche
over. Otherwise nothing doing. Hear we
are transferred to M.T.C. [Motor Transport
Corps.] We are much disgusted.

The German People Offers Peace.

The new German democratic government has this programme:

"The will of the people is the highest law."

The German people wants quickly to end the slaughter.
The new German popular government therefore has offered an

Armistice

and has declared itself ready for

Peace

on the basis of justice and reconciliation of nations.

It is the will of the German people that it should live in peace with all peoples, honestly and loyally.

What has the new German popular government done so far to put into practice the will of the people and to prove its good and upright intentions?

a) The new German government has appealed to President Wilson to bring about peace.

It has recognized and accepted all the principles which President Wilson proclaimed as a basis for a general lasting peace of justice among the nations.

b) The new German government has solemnly declared its readiness to evacuate Belgium and to restore it.

c) The new German government is ready to come to an honest understanding with France about.

Alsace-Lorraine.

d) The new German government has restricted the **U-boat War.**

No passengers steamers not carrying troops or war material will be attacked in future.

e) The new German government has declared that it will withdraw all German troops back over the German frontier.

f) — The new German government has asked the Allied Governments to name commissioners to agree upon the practical measures of the evacuation of Belgium and France.

These are the deeds of the new German popular government. Can these be called mere words, or bluff, or propaganda?

Who is to blame, if an armistice is not called now?

Who is to blame if daily thousands of brave soldiers needlessly have to shed their blood and die?

Who is to blame, if the hitherto undestroyed towns and villages of France and Belgium sink in ashes?

Who is to blame, if hundreds of thousands of unhappy women and children are driven from their homes to hunger and freeze?

The German people offers its hand for peace.

Propaganda leaflet dropped on Roy's camp (Sampigny)
October 29, 1918.
See his note on the English language side

Le peuple allemand offre la paix.

Le nouveau gouvernement démocratique de l'Allemagne agit en conformité avec le principe: »La volonté du peuple est la loi suprême«.

Le peuple allemand veut amener une fin rapide des massacres.
Le nouveau gouvernement du peuple allemand a pour cette raison offert

l'armistice

et s'est déclaré prêt à une

paix

du droit et de la conciliation des peuples.
C'est la volonté du peuple allemand de vivre honnêtement et loyalement en paix avec tous les autres peuples.
Le nouveau gouvernement du peuple allemand qu'a-t-il fait jusqu'à présent pour réaliser la volonté du peuple et pour prouver ses bonnes intentions sincères?

A) Le nouveau gouvernement allemand a demandé au président Wilson d'amener la paix.
Il a expressément reconnu et accepté les principes que le président Wilson a proclamés comme la base d'une paix de droit générale et durable parmi les peuples.

B) Le nouveau gouvernement allemand s'est solennellement déclaré prêt à

évacuer et dédommager la Belgique.

C) Le nouveau gouvernement allemand veut en toute loyauté s'accorder avec la France au sujet de

l'Alsace-Lorraine.

D) Le gouvernement allemand a modifié la guerre sous-marine en ce sens que des à présent les vapeurs servant au transport des voyageurs ne peuvent plus être attaqués, pour autant qu'ils ne transportent pas des troupes ou du matériel de guerre.

E) Le nouveau gouvernement allemand a déclaré vouloir retirer toutes les troupes allemandes derrière les frontières allemandes.

F) Le nouveau gouvernement allemand a demandé aux gouvernements adversaires, de constituer des négociateurs pour s'accorder au sujet de la réalisation pratique de l'évacuation de la Belgique et de la France.

Voilà ce que le nouveau gouvernement du peuple allemand a fait!
Y peut-on voir des phrases creuses? Est-ce là du bluff ou de la propagande!
A qui la faute, si dans ces circonstances l'armistice ne sera pas conclu?
A qui la faute, si tous les jours des milliers de braves soldats verseront encore leur sang et tomberont sous les balles?
A qui la faute, si les villes et les villages de la Belgique et de la France qui ont échappé jusqu'à présent à la destruction, tomberont en ruines?
A qui la faute, si des centaines de milliers de femmes malheureuses et d'enfants seront chassés de leurs domiciles et exposés à la famine et au froid?

Le peuple allemand tend la main pour la paix.

. . . and the French Side

Nov. 1, 1918
[SAMPIGNY]

Dear Everybody,

My first year is about finished, isn't it? This war has certainly lasted a lot longer than we thot possible a year ago. I don't see how "la guerre" can last much longer, tho, do you? The last few days everything is looking better. We all hope it will be over soon. I don't particularly love this kind of life.

I am still juggling boxes and lumber. Don't know when a change will come, and am not so crazy about mechanical work at this season anyway. Steel can get pretty cold, and gloves are not practical. No heat either.

The weather the last week has been just like it was last fall when Dad and I were in the Okanogan country. Cold clear nights freezes a little and bright sunny days. To-day has been cool and cloudy all day, and there are signs of rain this evening. So far we have had practically no rain in this camp. It seems to be a much better wet weather camp than the last one. It is nearly all paved, and drains well besides. So when we get the mud cleared off the streets the place will be all right. There is no place yet to buy any thing, so we are all saving our money. I miss the Y very much, but I think there will be one here soon. If not, a Salvation Army or something else that serves the same purpose.

We have the best quarters here I have had for a long time. Quartered in a big store building. The place is dry, clean and ventilated, also has a good tight floor. There are bunks for 22 men, but only about 15 here, so we have plenty of room. Our heating plant is a stove which once toasted Fritzie's shins. We got it, also some chairs and tables, out of the old German trenches. We've never run out of wood yet, because there is plenty in camp, and we spent a month at Camp Hancock, where we learned many things. Water about 20 feet from our door, and only 30 yards to the mess hall. So, altogether, it is a pretty good place.

It is nice that the Buckskin Swede finally got married. I'm sorry for the poor soldier, but I suppose after a man has soldiered in this country for three or four years he can stand anything. It must be so, or he never would have pulled such a stunt.

I went to the trenches Sunday afternoon, but as I only had half a day I didn't get to see much. It's about a seven mile hike to the beginning of them, and as we had to get out on the roads before dark, we didn't have but about 30 minutes to look around. And we never got to the real trenches at all. There are some where Fritz had hospitals, workshops, etc. all underground. Some of the boys have been up there, but I've never had the opportunity. I'm looking forward to Sunday again.

I've run out of anything to say, so guess I'll quit.

Love to everybody,

— Roy

Sgt. R. E. Thompson

Co 13, 1st Air Serv. Mech. Rgt.

American E. F.

DIARY

Tue 5
Nothing new or startling except news. The prospect of a finish is causing a good deal of excitement.

Wed 6
Same old job, with which I am getting much disgusted.

Thur 7
Again the same. Rained nearly all day.
Lots of peace talk, and everybody is
figuring on when they will be home.

Fri 8
Transferred to motor shop. Much better
job. Cloudy but not much rain.

Sat 9
Working on Ford bearings. Rainy day.
German envoys trying to negotiate with
Foch.

Nov 8, '18

Dear Everybody at home:

There's so much argument going on here that I don't know whether I can write or not. There being no place to go around here the bunch stays in at night and argues about every subject under the sun. Of course, when they get excited this place is so noisy writing is impossible.

I got a new job to-day. Was sent to the motor shop. On all the overhaul jobs the motor comes out and goes to the motor shop. So we will work on nothing else. Similar departments handle electrical work, tire work, etc. It looks to me like the best job around here. I know it is a much better place to work in than the main shops. The building is better, we have more tools, more light and cleaner work. I narrowly escaped getting a good job this morning. I didn't get the order to report to the motor dept. until late, so reported about 7:45 instead of 7:00. When I reported the foreman told me there was nothing to do just then, then asked me if I knew anything about motors. I had to admit that I was supposed to know a little. He asked me some more questions, then told me that the officer in charge of the power plant was leaving for a few days and they had to have somebody to watch the engines. (Two big stationary gasoline engines, running the generators which light the camp) So we went over and found that an engineer was already on the job. So the delayed order cost me a nice soft job. It was some job, too. Nothing to do but sit around and watch engines and boss a couple of fellows who probably knew more about the job than I did.

We have had cool showery weather the past week. Not much rain, yet, but enough to make the camp a little muddy as they were at the other camp, for which we are truly thankful. I don't appreciate wading sixteen inches of mud like anybody ought to who lives in this country.

Only got a half day off Sunday instead of the full day I was hoping for. Went to the trenches but of course didn't have time to reach the best of them. However, what I saw was well worth the trouble. Whatever time I have next Sunday is going to be spent the same way.

It's bedtime for me. Bon Nuit.

Love to all of you,

— Roy

We're supposed to be transferred to the M.T.C. (Motor Transport Corp.) Don't know whether our address will change or not.

Sgt. R. E. Thompson
Co. 13, 1st A.S. Mech. Regt.
American E. F.

CHAPTER 3
The War Ends

DIARY

Sunday November 10, 1918
Cool foggy day. Worked half day.
Commissary opened up after dinner.
Raided it and got some jam and candy.
Beaucoup mail.

Monday November 11, 1918
Cool day. No rain. Rumor says armistice
was signed last night and hostilities
stopped at 11 A.M. Unconfirmed.

Tue 12
Learned that armistice was really signed.
Everybody is highly pleased.
"When do we go home?" Coldest night we
have had.

Wed 13
Fine clear day, but cold. Got off from 10
until noon. Truck shop afternoon. Clear
moonlight night.

Thur 14
Business as usual. Back in motor shop and
lots of work.

Fri 15
Clear sunny and cold. No particular
excitement. Cold night.

Sat 16
Beaucoup cold. Ice lasted all day. Ground
stayed frozen also cloudy. Some breeze.
Lapping Ford pistons.

Nov 16, 1918 *[SAMPIGNY]*

Dear Everybody:

Just woke up to the fact that I haven't written for over a week. Had intended writing some letters last night; also the night before; but in both cases came in and sat down by the fire and thereafter lacked the ambition. Things are going fine now. Weather is great – no rain for over a week now. The nights are clear cold moonlight. Days have been warm but to-day was cloudy and chilly all day. Ice hasn't melted all day, the ground softened a little. It seems just like November at home.

I am liking this camp better all the time. No retreat and no reveille. Get up any time you feel like it. Just so you get to work on time is all that is required. Quarters are good, and chow is the best since I left Camp Lewis. We have been getting jam and hot biscuits, which before have at times been rather scarce. Also lots of good fresh beef. Haven't seen any corned willy for nearly a month.

My job is coming fine. Wednesday I ran out of a job about 9:30 and the foreman told me to get out of sight until noon. This I accordingly did, and when I came back after noon there was still no work, so they sent me to the truck shop. In the meantime a bunch of motors came in and I have been busy ever since. I am working on nothing but Fords. I like it fine, and hope they leave me there as long as we're doing this kind of work.

I am going to send some more Stars and Stripes when I can get them and can get the necessary paper to wrap them in.

So you think I've been "worrying" about that allotment, do you? Well, you had better guess again. I don't worry about anything. Do a good deal of thinking sometimes, but worrying is out of my line. I knew the money would be all right, anyway. You see, it happened like this: When the boys first went to camp, there was a great deal of misunderstanding about the allotment business. So lots of the boys made voluntary allotments because they thot it was required, or would be. Later they learned differently, and began to try to get the allotments cancelled. There was so much of this that a ruling was made to cancel all voluntary allotments. A special form was put out, and all voluntary allotments to be renewed were made out on this form and sent in to H.Q. I fixed mine as soon as XXXXXXed about the new *XXXXXXXXXXXXX I knew your money would come sometimes even if it was delayed somewhat.

In the last letters I got you say "some people think the war will be over in a few months, but I don't". What do you think about it now? I rather believe peace will be signed by Christmas. It may not be for a long time after that, of course. Still I have hopes that they will get things settled by that time. Are you still afraid I'll get to flying and break my neck? I think you can rest on that score now.

My think tank is dry. Guess I'd better quit and XXXXXXXX.

— Roy
Sgt R. E. Thompson
Co 13. 1st A. S. Mech Regt.
American E. F.

* *The XXXX in this letter are in place of missing words. The letter looked like a mouse had chewed on one corner*

DIARY

Sun 17
Cloudy and cold. East wind. Worked
half day. Afternoon Griner, xxxx, and I
went to trenches. Didn't see much. Got on
wrong road. Came back by Aprremont,
St. Agnant, Marbothe and Mecrin. [This
identifies the south face of the St Mihiel salient.]

Mon 18
As usual, fliver motors. Clear and cold.

Tue 19
The same. Capt. made us a talk at
6:30. Leaving the company, perhaps
permanently, and made a few remarks.

Wed 20
New Lieut. on job. Made us a speech on
neatness and "military courtesy". Shoes
at 45° angle, etc. Trouble with rations. No
bread, and feeding us biscuits.

Nov. 20, 18.

Dear Homefolks:

I wrote to Dorma a couple of nights ago, so haven't much news to write. I am feeling fine. Haven't had a sick day in three months. If there is any "flu" or anything else serious in camp I haven't heard of it. It is too bad you are having so much trouble with it there. I was very sorry to hear of Warren Clare's death. He was a splendid fellow. I certainly hope they succeed in getting that disease checked soon. Our captain was sent away a day or two ago. Don't know whether he will come back or not, but hope so. Our commanding officer now is a lieut. who has been in France about a week. He called us out to-night and gave us a talk on saluting and keeping our bunks neat and so on. He doesn't realize that this is France, and that conditions are vastly different.

As I told Dorma, I was up in the trenches Sunday. Was up beyond St. Mihiel and intend to go still farther next Sunday, as I can go where I want to without getting lost now. If there are any small articles you are especially interested in, let me know and if possible I'll collect the same. Lugers and officers' spiked helmets are the favorite souvenirs, but both are very scarce. Bayonets and gas masks are also quite popular. The Luger is all I have. No belt or holster yet, but am trying to get them. Got some ammunition yesterday. Think I'll have to try the gun on Sunday.

Weather is fine now. To-night is a fine clear moonlight light. Freezes a little nights, but has thawed out again every day except last Friday.

We work 7 to 11:45 and 1 to 5. Also half a day on Sunday. Of this there is absolutely no need, so far as I can see. About all our fellows are in the shops or driving truck now, and a gang of Boche are doing the stevedore work.

It is 9:30 and I have written all I know that I dare to write. The rest I'll tell you some other time.

Bon nuit,   — Roy

Sgt. R. E. Thompson

Co 13, 1st A.S.Mech Regt.

American E. F.

DIARY

Thursday, Nov. 21
Biscuits three times today - a military
event unparalled in modern warfare.
Twisted my ankle and am limping
somewhat.

Fri 22
Sick call. Stayed in quarters and soaked
my foot in hot water.

Sat 23
Worked again. Ankle sore but usable.
Moving motor shop into another building.

Sun 24
Went to trenches at 10 with Wisdom,
Swezey and Fowler. Rained on us on way
back. Lunch in St Mihiel. Dad's Xmas
letter day.

The envelope for this next letter was addressed to Mr. G. A. Thompson, and in the "stamp" corner was written "Father's Xmas Letter".

SAMPIGNY, MEUSE, NOV 23, 1918

My Dear Dad:

As everybody on both sides of the pond is supposed to know, we are requested to write a special letter to-morrow. The censor is almost out of a job, so a little history of what I have been doing the last year may prove interesting. And as I don't know what I'll be doing to-morrow, I'm going to write it to-night.

Guess you don't know much about where I have been since I was at Camp Merritt. We left there early Feb 8, and by noon were on board the President Lincoln, formerly a German freighter. That night we moved out into the harbor, where we stayed until the night of the 10th. Moved out after dark, and the next land we saw were some islands off the coast of France, fourteen days later. That afternoon, the 24th, we anchored in the harbor of St. Nazaire. Landed the 26th. Marched about two miles to camp. We stayed here a month, but did practically nothing except drill. I haven't the exact dates of our movements for about six weeks after this. Our next move was to Blois, on the Loire River above St. Nazaire. Here about a week, then to Gondrecourt. If you can get a large map of France you will find Gondrecourt in the extreme southern part of Meuse. Two miles north of there, at Abainville, is where we built the railroad and railroad repair shops during April, May and early June. From here we went to Langres, Haute Marne. (Upper Marne) I think I told you about visiting the source of the Marne, and other interesting things near Langres.

In late July we went back to Abainville for a week. The narrow-guage line to Corcy was then finished, or nearly so, and in operation. As you know, we went back to Langres and our auto work.

The next move landed us here. If you can find a map that shows Commercy and St. Mihiel you will find us about half-way between, at a little town called Sampigny. This is an old French cavalry camp. We have converted the stables to shops.

That the past year has been the most wonderful of my experience goes without saying. Tho time has dragged at times, still, as I look back over the year the time seems short. This is especially true of the last six months, since I have been very busy ever since April, and haven't had time hanging on my hands any. Of course, I was lonesome and homesick the first few weeks, but I soon made friends and got settled into army ways. And now, tho I don't like the life, I am enjoying myself, feeling fine, and haven't a thing in the world to worry about. It is the general opinion that we will be here only a few months more, possibly only a few weeks. Of course we know nothing about it, and it is possible we will be attached to the Third army, which would mean quite a lengthy stay here. Somebody will have to stay, of course, but I think the chances are the other way, decidedly.

So be getting ready for another big trip, and some of these days we'll be doctoring the old jitney up and be heading for the wilds again.

It may seem at times like I have forgotten you, Dad, but I haven't, and I think you understand me, perhaps better than anyone else does. Many and many a time I've wished that you could be with me, but of course that can't be.

There is no chance of being with you this Christmas, tho I'd certainly like to be. So I'll just wish you health and happiness, and the best of Christmases.

— Roy
Sgt R. E. Thompson
Co 13. 1st A. S. Mech Regt.
American E. F.

Roy's Souvenir Cup ... 75 mm shell

DIARY

Mon Nov. 25
Finished moving shop and got settled
down to work again. Rainy day.

Tue 26
Nothing exciting. Plenty of rain. Ankle is
pretty sore but getting better.

Wed 27
As usual, it is raining. New bunch moved
into the billet.

Thur 28
No work. Swezey and I went hiking and
got some shells, etc. Big (!) dinner. Made
souvenirs all afternoon. So busy I forgot
supper.

Fri 29
New men came into shop and the old crew
were separated and put with new men.
Had cootie inspection at noon. "Shirts off"

Sat 30
Applied for pass to Verdun. Cold cloudy
day.

Sun Dec 1
Got up at 4:45 to catch 5:30 train, which
came at 7. Dugny at 10, hiked to Verdun,
and took in the sights. Back to camp at
8:15. Cold and cloudy.

SAMPIGNY DEC 2, 1918

Dear Sis Vella:

    I've written to both the other kids since I wrote to you, so you
get this one. You shouldn't, tho, because I've got two or three letters from Leola since I got one from you. Next time you'd better

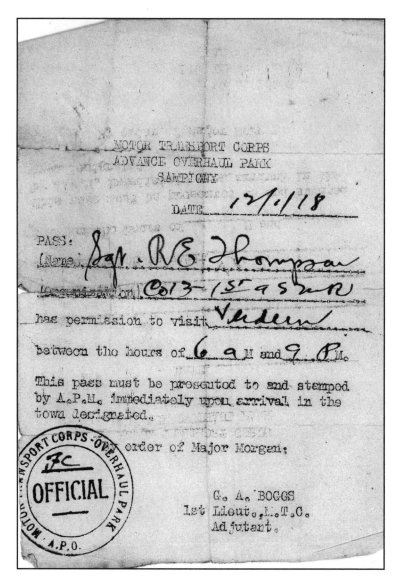

MOTOR TRANSPORT CORPS
ADVANCE OVERHAUL PARK
SAMPIGNY

DATE _12/1/18_

PASS:
(Name) _Sgt. R.E. Thompson_

(organization) _Co 13 - 1st 4 S.T.R._

has permission to visit _Verdun_

between the hours of _6 a_ M and _9_ P.M.

This pass must be presented to and stamped
by A.P.M. immediately upon arrival in the
town designated.

By order of Major Morgan;

G. A. BOGGS
1st Lieut., M.T.C.
Adjutant.

Roy's one day pass to visit Verdun....

write if you want a letter.

I got paid a few minutes ago. Drew 161.50f. I used to draw
169.50 last spring. French money is coming up it seems. I got
up yesterday morning at 4:45, got my breakfast, and got ready

to catch the 5:30 train. It came all right – about seven. Five of us went. It was cold work waiting for the train, and still colder riding on it. It had no windows, or almost none, and no fire. It took three hours to run 45 kilometers. When we got off we started hiking rather than wait in the cold. Hoofed it five miles into Verdun. Got in a little before noon, ate our lunch and started in to see the town. It is pretty thoroly shot up. Parts of it are untouched; other parts are the worst ruins I have ever seen. Not even a wall standing. We took in the sights in town, but didn't have time to go to the battlefield, which was about four miles further. Wish I could have. Caught a truck back to our railroad station, got out at 6:10 and back to camp a little after 8. It was rather a chilly trip, but I've seen Verdun. So I guess it was worth it.

Tell Leola I will write in a few days. And you'd better do likewise.

Love to the whole family,

— Roy

Sgt. R. E. Thompson

Co 13   1st A. S. M. Regt.

American E. F.

DIARY

Mon Dec. 2
Back in shop at same old job. Got paid
161.50 francs. Y opened up for business.

Tues 3
Rainy. Working on a Ford outdoors.
Burned brgs. Worked on souvenirs after
supper.

Verdun Ruins

Wed 4
Same job. Souvenirs again after supper.

Thur 5
Warm and rainy. Changed from flivers
[Ford Model-Ts] to Dodges. Assembling on
factory plan.

SAMPIGNY, DEC 5, 1918

Dear Home-folks:

Well, how is everything on the farm this evening? This is a nice warm rainy night. It has been raining more or less the last four days, but is not cold. Sunday was rather chilly.

There is not a thing to write about. I have had no mail for several days. Over two weeks ago I got a few letters dated Oct. 25. Have rec'd several since, all of earlier date. So some day soon I ought to get a bunch of them. We are on the same work we've been on for a month. No change except I changed from flivvers to Dodges to-day. Rather glad of it because I had been on Fords for a month, and was getting rather tired of them. Besides, I may need all the Dodge knowledge I have and can gain before I get the old bus at home in working order. I have been working the last two nights. Voluntary extra work.

There has been a lot of talk lately about moving. It seems to have blown-over now, tho, so guess we will be here for a while yet.

Guess I'd just as well quit, as I've nothing to write. Hope you haven't the flu yet. I'm feeling fine.

— Roy

DIARY

Fri Dec 6
Assembling Dodge

Sat 7
Finished Dodges and back to flivers.
Drilled 12:40 to 1:00

Sun 8
Inspection and drill. I worked instead.
Swezey and I went after shell rings. Found
three dead Boche. Electrified the door
after I got back. Beaucoup fun.

Mon 9
No excitement.

Tues 10
Rainy. Bought a helmet. Generally quiet.

Wed 11
Rainy, nothing to report on the Sampigny front.

DEC 11, 1918

Dear Homefolks:

Well, how goes everything? I am quite as usual feeling fine. Have only a very slight cold but no sign of sore throat or flu.

We have been getting a lot of rain lately. It is clear and moonlight to-night. Haven't seen a flake of snow yet and very little ice – none at all for two weeks.

We started drilling Saturday. Drill daily from 12:40 to 1:00 and 1-1/2 hours on Sundays. It is not much time, but will probably improve us a little. Probably if we keep at it long enough we will learn to march passably.

Went hiking again Sunday afternoon. Went a different way, and found some very interesting things without going nearly so far as usual. Didn't find anything of value tho we found lots of old rifles, helmets, and such junk. The back areas are being salvaged now, and I suppose the front line trenches will be before long. They gather up all the old junk. Some of it is very dangerous, especially the unexploded shells and hand grenades. We don't know anything about such articles, so we don't practice taking them apart to see how they are made. Several guys have tried that and started something. One blew off four fingers and I don't know what happened to the others. They went to the hospital.

After I got in Sunday night we had a lot of fun. Took a Ford coil and storage battery and connected it to the door handle and the wet ground. When a guy took hold of the handle he'd jump as high as the house. It's the regular spark-plug jolt and is pretty heavy when a fellow is not expecting it. We caught a lot of them. Some would come in mad enough to beat us up and some would grin and pretend they never felt it.

Eighteen fellows from here are going to Luxemburg to-morrow. There are 850 German trucks there to be put in running order. I suppose they will come back to this base for overhauling as rapidly as possible. Three or four of the eighteen are from this company. Wish I was one of them. Hope to get into Germany some time anyway, unless they start us the other way.

Don't know anything more of interest to-night.

Love to all of you   — Roy

DIARY

Thur Dec 12
Rainy. No drill

Fri 13
Drilled in platoons for review purposes.

Sat 14
Same kind of performing as yesterday.

Sun 15   Had the grand review. Sunshiny
forenoon. Cloudy after. Went with Griner

*to trenches. Beaucoup Boche. Dorland
took our pictures.*

*Well, how are you tonight? What do you think of my stationery? I
fished it out of a dugout today. Have no news, but will write a letter
soon anyway. Everything is proceeding quite as usual. Roy*

Mon 16
Colder and rainy.

Tue 17
Rainy. Got my Xmas package.

Wed 18
No excitement. Rainy and windy.

Thur 19
The same. Few letters.

Fri 20
Lots of rain and some wind. 20 minutes
drill.

Sat 21
Not much rain. Had platoon drill with Co. 7.

Sun 22
Platoon drill again. Made souvenirs.

Mon 23
Rainy. No drill.

Tue 24
First snow of the season after supper.
Issued Y parcels and Q.M. candy.

Dec 23, 1918

Dear Sis:

I'm totally out of a job to-night, so I'm going to write a few lines. It's after nine o'clock, which is late for a lot of these guys, as they've gone to bed. I just came back from the bath-house and have neglected to put on complete uniform as yet. Don't suppose that makes any difference, tho, does it?

Say, if you think Pullman is dull, or ever was, I wish you could drop into this place for a week or two. Bingville, by comparison, leads a gay and giddy life. I've been here since Oct 21, and haven't been to any kind of a meeting or a show in that time. There are shows here, but so many attend that you have to go an hour early to get a seat. I don't relish that, and don't care a great deal for movies anyhow, so haven't gone once. And yet, in spite of the dullness, time is simply flying. My work is interesting, instructive and useful, and that is something to be thankful for, anyway.

I have had only one letter from you, one from mother, and one from Lottie in the last two weeks, so don't know any more than I did the last time I wrote you. The candy came thru in grand shape and believe me, it was the best thing I have tasted in many moons. In humble acknowledgement, I'm going to send you a paper-weight of rather substantial construction. I think it will look quite nifty on your desk. And I solemnly assure you it is the genuine article.

You asked me a lot of questions about how we acted. As I told you before, most of the excitement was over there. Seems strange, but raised no excitement at all. Don't imagine there will be much when peace is signed. The Air Service seems to be going home. Their work, of course, is finished. We (Cos. 7, 8, 9, and 13th, 1st A.S.M.R. *[Air Service Mechanics Regiment]* and 7, 8, 9 ,10, 4TH A.S.M.R.) are attached to the M.T.C. *[Motor Transport Corp .]*

We may be started home next week, or we may be attached to the Third Army and kept here indefinitely. We don't know anything definite at all. Of course, the air is full of wild rumors, but they have no weight, and nobody believes them. I don't like to hang crape, but it's entirely possible we will stay over some months yet. Most of us expect to get back in the spring, but that opinion won't put us there. The M.T.C. has an enormous amount of work ahead of it, and if they hang onto us -------.

Everybody else is in bed, and I guess I'd better do likewise. Write often and lots.

— Roy

Sgt. R. E. Thompson   266969
Co 13, 1st A.S.Mech. Regt.
American E. F.

Put on the number, sil vous plait.

DIARY

Wed. Dec. 25
Snowed nearly all day. Griner and I
went to trenches. Too much snow to
find anything. Came back to major's
dugout, made a fire and warmed up.

[The following letter is mildly damaged from mice or abrasion.....Corners of several pages are missing. Where it is obvious what he was writing the words have been inserted....If there is a question I have inserted XXX.]

SAMPIGNY, MEUSE
CHRISTMAS DAY '18

Merry Christmas everybody!

Well, how are you enjoying yourselves to-day?   As usual I suppose with enough good eats to feed a company. I don't envy you any, but wish I was there to get my share.

We started our Xmas celebration last night with a neat little snowstorm. Melted as it fell here, but piled up a little on the surrounding hills. The place was pretty noisy until about midnight. Then this morning we stayed in bed until we got ready to get up. (First time since Aix *[le Bain]*) I rose sometime between daylight and noon. Too late for breakfast but got "punk" and coffee. Had plenty of jam and toasted my bread, XXX fare badly at all. Then Griner and I headed "a la trenchee". There was no snow in camp, but we struck it as soon as we hit the higher ground, and the further we went the more snow we struck. Got back to where it was about two inches deep and still coming, when we gave XXX up as a bad job. Came back to a first-class dugout; formerly inhabited by a major. It was a cozy little place, perfectly dry, and with a fireplace, curtained windows, and other modern fixtures. We steamed up said fireplace, toasted our bread and our shins, and dried our shoes. Then dined on toast, jam and chocolate. We had a very good day. They had no special dinner at camp. Had pie extra – don't know what else. Thanksgiving Day they took 5 francs from the mess fund for each man and bought fresh pork. They cost 45¢ a lb. on the foot. How would you like to sell a few swine at that? Nobody was satisfied with the Thanksgiving dinner. For a dollar apiece extra we should have gotten a good feed, but didn't. So this time they just put out the regular feed, with what trimmings they could put on without paying extra for them. The mess fund I spoke of belongs to the company. It is money we saved. You know, so much (42¢ a day per man, I think.) is allowed in the U.S.

We didn't draw that much at Hancock and Merritt, so the company has some money of its own. Over here the stuff is not handled that way, and you get the same as the other fellow. No chance to save money. You asked me a whole lot of questions about what I'm going to do. I don't know, and won't until I get home and see how things are. I suppose I have six months after discharge to get on my land. Am not certain about it. One thing is sure – I'm not going to tour France. The U.S. for me, as soon as I can get there. I intend to hold that land to a finish and prepare XXXXXX college. That's the only definite plans I have now. Have a million wild schemes in my head. Don't suppose any of them will ever hatch. As I don't know how things will be when I get home, or at what season I will arrive, XXXXX is possible to XXXrm an definite XXXns. I think you can XXXXX that. If there is anything in particular you want, let me know what it is and I'll be thinking it over.

We don't know anything about when we will be home. Perhaps next week; perhaps next year. We, or most of us, think it will be within two or three months. We are not even sure whether we are in the Air Service or the Motor Transport Corp. This latter has the biggest job of any branch of the army, and if we are transferred to it (as seems possible) we might stay several months. Don't worry about little things like that, anyway. I'm getting along "puffickly". I've stood this country 10 months, guess I can stand a few more. It's 10:30, I must quit. Happy New Year, all of you!

— Roy

Sgt R. E. Thompson 266969

Co 13, 1st A. S. Mechs Regt.

American E. F.

[Written vertically in the left side of the last page of this letter was : "Lots of R. E. Thompson's in XXXX" It appears that Roy was advising the "Homefolks" to use his serial number as part of his address. Interestingly, the return address on the outside of the envelope read: "Sgt. R. E. Thompson U.S. Army"]

DIARY

Thur Dec 26
Cold and windy. Trying to snow. Platoon
drill.

Fri 27
Cold day. Company drill.

Sat 28
Warmer and raining all day.

Sun 29
Raining. Inspection but too rainy to drill.
Made souvenirs all afternoon.

Mon 30
Beaucoup rain, and that's all. No
excitement whatsoever.

Tue 31
Rainy and windy.

Wed Jan 1, 1919
Got up quite late and hiked to Commercy
with Ole W. Bought some junk.

Thur. 2
Rainy. 10th Co. 2nd Regt. Men came to shop.
Some mail. Issued our monthly allowance
of francs.

SAMPIGNY, FRANCE
JAN 1, 1919

Happy New Year and a better one next time!

What have you been doing to-day, and what kind of a time did you have? I presume the usual New Year's dance happened. I intended to go to mass last night with another curious guy, but we got sleepy and backed out. Went to bed instead. At midnight a regular barrage broke lose, rifles, automatics and star shells. (They are fired from a large gun, resembling a shot gun.) There must have been twenty guys at least trying to see how fast they could burn rifle ammunition. Several automatic pistols, and a machine gun or automatic rifle --- couldn't tell which. They sure raised a fuss for about half an hour. By that time some officers were on the job, arresting the celebrators. Several of them got pinched. Don't know whether they've been released or not.

Got up about eight this morning and went to Commercy just before noon. Got some stationery and other stuff. Couldn't get a diary, tho I tried every place in town. If you can stick one in a letter it will be much appreciated. A small one – something like Mamie sent last year is the best. I will put my records in a notebook temporarily.

Am mailing you a large map of France and some large views of Douremy. They are not bad, tho hardly what I would have selected if I had had any choice in the matter. The map is marked, every place I have been stationed, also the towns where I stopped while on leave.

I have no news and Ole is waiting for his pen, so will quit.

Love to all of you.

— Roy
Sgt R. E. Thompson 266969
Co 13, 1st A. S. Mech. Regt.
American E. F.

The preceeding return address appeared both at the bottom of the letter, and on the outside of the envelope. The cease fire is in place, and the troops are just now getting serious about including a serial number in the mailing address.

CHAPTER 4

The Accident

On Sunday, the 5th of January, Roy was involved in a railway accident, severely injuring his right foot. His diary entries for the next few days are all in the same clear handwriting, apparently always using the same fountain pen. Under the circumstances, I surmise that he did some catching up after he received his personal belongings. In a previous letter he had asked for a new pocket diary. The 1918 diary carries no manufacturer's I.D., but has a page of U.S. postal rates. The new one has only a printed number inside back flyleaf: 3056-1/2.

DIARY

Sunday Jan 5, 1919
Griner and I started to Abainville on bicycles. Train accident at 2:10. Taken to Gondrecourt hospital and immediate operation.

Mon 6
Lots of pain. Morphine before I could sleep.

Tue 7
More pain. Wound dressed A.M. Foot amputated about 3 P.M. Lots of pain after I came out of ether. Finally morphine and some sleep.

Wed 8
Very restless. One dressing that made me take notice.

Thur 9
Began feeding me. Same was much appreciated.

Sun 12
Stormy. F.G. *[Frank Griner?]* stopped a few minutes on way to Langres. S.A. *[Salvation Army]* people in.

Sun 19
Griner and Davis came down with my property. Also letters. Very glad to see them and to get the stuff. S.A. come in every Sunday with doughnuts.

Sun 26
Past week has been cold and snowy. Looked for Griner, but he didn't come. S.A. in as usual.

Mon 27
Doctor tells me I am going to base *[hospital]*. Leg coming beautifully.

Tue 28
Moved to B.H. 45 *[Base Hospital]* at Toul. Roads rough, but rode without much discomfort.

Back to Roy's letters, which are upbeat for a young man who has just lost a foot.

IN HOSPITAL 1/15/19
[GONDRECOURT]

Dear Mother:

Well, I'm still here. This is some place – just like drawing a pension. I am free from any pain of consequence now. Still have some, of course, but not the knock out kind. So I'm doing fine, sleeping like a baby and eating like "Old Can"*. Have no idea when I'll go out of here. This is the second pen I've tried and both are dry, so I guess I'll have to quit. No mail since I came here – ten days ago.

— Love, Roy

*"Old Can" was the family's milk cow.

This letter was written on Red Cross stationery, bore a censors stamp and signature, and had the full return address both inside and on the envelope.

GONDRECOURT, FRANCE
MON., JAN 20, '19

Dear Mother, Dad and the rest:

Well, I'm feeling better this morning. A couple of the boys came down on a motorcycle yesterday. Brot my toilet articles, personal property (towels, books, etc.) and two letters. That helped mightily. I read Dad's letter without a bit of difficulty, and glad I was to get it. Also they told me some good news. That the M.T.C. *[Motor Transport Corp]* didn't succeed in transferring us to that outfit; that the company is thru work Feb 1; and that they expect to start home soon after that. So it looks like I'd be home in a couple of months after all. How does that strike you?

This is the most wonderful ink I ever tried to use. The pen doesn't feed fast enough, either.

I think it advisable to discontinue production in the correspondence dept, as I don't think the letters you would write in future could reach me. You might transfer the personnel and equipment to the Pie Production Dept. and endeavor to attain maximum production in that line by April 1, and sooner if possible. I am quite sure that from now until I get home my movements will be so frequent and uncertain that letters never would catch me. If there is anything of importance happens you can write.

The Salvation Army people come around every Sunday afternoon. Have a little talk and a few songs. Then they come around and visit every bed, chat with the fellows a little, and distribute cookies and doughnuts. A man from the Red Cross comes around every day with newspapers and cigarettes, nuts, chewing gum and such dope. I have no kick to make on the care I'm getting. I am getting along fine. Progress seems slow to me, but the doctor says its <u>very</u> satisfactory. So I guess I ought to be satisfied.

I'm going to quit. This pen is too bum for any use.

— Roy
Ward A, Camp Hospital No. 1
Gondrecourt

Was very sad to hear G.W. was sick. Hope he has recovered ere this.

— Roy

I find the contents of this letter incredible. Roy is talking about getting back to his unit and returning to the U.S. Three weeks earlier he had had a foot amputated. We learned from Roy's sister, Leola 75 years after this event, that infection followed the original amputation operation. Lacking antibiotics, the medical team returned him to the operating table several times during these early weeks. Each time they would remove the infected tissue and shorten the remaining bone below the knee. The final amputation was about midway between the knee and the ankle. We shall never know if Roy really believed he could return to duty as a mechanic and travel home with his unit, or if he was merely blowing smoke for the benefit of his parents.

GONDRECOURT, JAN **25** *[1919]*

Dear Everybody:

Well, I haven't written for four or five days, so guess I'll try it again, just to let you know that I'm still thriving.

I am getting acquainted with the hospital force and all the older patients in this ward. They are mostly surgical cases; some non-contagious medical. They are a good-natured gang. More than half are convalescent; take care of themselves, feed the bed patients, carry in the wood and sweep the floor. Of course, while a man is sick he gets fine care. I find this place much better than the stories I had heard of army hospitals had led me to expect. The surgeons and doctors are certainly doing good work, and the nurses are good, too.

There was a sad case came in here Tuesday evening. In a French family living near here there were eight sons. Seven were in the army, one of them being killed. The other was twelve years old. One of the soldier brothers came home on furlough, and the boy got hold of his automatic and, while playing with it, shot himself thru the abdomen. He was horribly torn up and bled a great deal internally. There was no French surgeon near, so he was put into an American ambulance and brot here. The officers here operated immediately. The operation required a long time, three hours at least it seemed to me. When they finished he was so weak from loss of blood that nobody expected him to live over two hours. He was still alive in the morning, tho, and that afternoon they decided that with more blood he had a fighting chance, tho a slim one. So about seven o'clock they started a blood-transfusion operation, one of the boys of the hospital force furnishing the blood. The shock was too much, tho, and he died that night at 1 o'clock. Everybody was sorry to see him go. He was certainly a plucky little chap and made a good fight. And he certainly had all the help that could be given him. There were two or three doctors working at each operation, and a nurse was with the boy every minute from the time he came in until he died.

We've been having winterish weather the past week. It's been freezing some, tho of course I don't know how much as I haven't been outside. Have had a few flurries of snow, but nothing of consequence.

I am still doing well. Am getting so I can move around considerable without any pain and I can lie in bed anyway I please. At first the ankle was so sensitive I had to lie a certain way all the time. That was more or less tiresome. Was up for two or three hours today, for the first time. It was quite a relief, believe me. The doctor hasn't given me any idea as to when I'll be fit for service again.

How is the flu? I got Dorma's letter of 12/24 couple of days ago, and she said everything was still closed.

Well, this is all I know to-day.

Love to all of you.   — Roy

Sgt. R. E. Thompson 266969
Ward A, Camp Hospital No. 1
A.P.O. 703, A.E.F,

Are you preserving the Stars and Stripes I send? I hope you are, because there are lots of things in them I want to read again, and others that I want to keep for reference; those division marking lists for example. I'm sending another to-day.

DIARY

Wed 29
B.H. 45 and patients transfer to B.H.
87. Hospital train came in, causing
considerable excitement. Chow is <u>punk.</u>

Thur 30
Changed to silver nitrate dressing.
Nothing of importance happened.

Fri 31
S.A. apples and oranges. Another dressing
with silver nitrate and iodine.

Sat Feb 1
S.A. came in with apples, oranges, razors,
soap, brushes and etc.

Sun 2
Got out on crutches for first time. It's a
great help. Ward master and guard had
lovely scrap about 9:30.

Mon 3
Nothing of importance occurred. Up a
good deal but pretty weak.

SGT. R. E. THOMPSON 266969
CO 13, 1ST A.S.MECH. REGT.
SAT. FEB 1, 1919

Dear Homefolks:

Well, I've landed in a new place since I wrote you. Am now in B.H. *[base hospital]* 82 at Toul. The other hospital was so crowded that the ones who were able to travel had to be moved to make room for cases requiring immediate attention. So a gang of us were shipped out. I moved by ambulance; about thirty miles. The road was frozen and rough, but I made the trip in fine shape and with no discomfort worth mentioning. I didn't believe I could do it. Guess the captain knew more about it than I did. This is a much larger place than the other hospital. They are taking splendid care of us. Haven't seen anybody from the company since I wrote last, so don't know any more about when I'll start back than I did then. The number of things a fellow doesn't know and can't find out in this army is simply wonderful.

The Salvation Army came in yesterday, distributing oranges and big red Wash. *[Washington state]* apples. The best thing I've tasted in eighty years. Wish they'd come every day.

Got a bunch of letters Monday, representing Mother, Mamie, Clara and Leola. I thot that was a pretty good family showing for one day. The dates ranged from 12/18 to 12/30. Was very glad to hear that G.W. was up and about again, as one of the preceding letters made me think he was pretty sick.

Sure wish I could have been with you Christmas, but it wasn't exactly convenient this time. Next time I get in this army it's going to be with the understanding that I go home whenever I want to and stay as long as I please.

Weather is still cool. Snow hasn't melted for over a week.

As I have a habit of doing, I've run out of news just as I got started in, so there's nothing to do but quit.

Love   — Roy

Later in the day. The S.A. people just came in again with more red apples and oranges. Also soap, shaving soap and brushes, safety razors and blades and matches. It was all good stuff, too, and everything free. And they finished up by coming around with a want book so they could bring each man everything he needed when they come around again. Pretty good, I call it. I have a new address:

Ward 280, B.H. 82
A.P.O. 784 American E. F.

DIARY

Tues Feb 4
S.A. around again. Devoted most of
afternoon to copying the ward book.

Wed 5
Nothing unusual except a shampoo. Real
snow storm in afternoon. First one since
Xmas.

Thur 6
Snowing. Miss Keene went on leave, so we
have a new nurse.

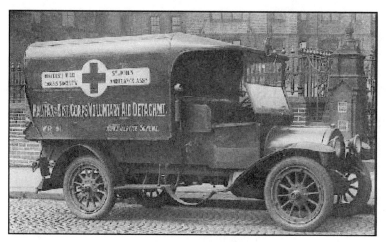

1916 Dodge army ambulance
[This one has balloon tires!]

Fri 7
Copying the ward book. Snowy forenoon,
sunny after. I am getting much stronger.
Walked to dressing room yesterday and
this morning.

Sat 8
Clear, sunny and cold. Took a "smear"
(germ test) of my wound.

Sun 9
Germ test favorable. Dr. says he will try to
operate tomorrow. Hope he does.

TOUL, FRANCE, B.H. 82, SUNDAY 2/9/19

Mine Much-honored Relatives,:

Since I should have written you three days ago and didn't, because, I presume, there was nothing in the world to hinder me, I will make what amends I may by writing now. I have rec'd no more mail since coming here so there's nothing to answer. And there certainly is nothing to write about. I used to think things were dull and unexciting in camp. Now I find they were hilarious to the extreme. I used to put in eight hours a day either working or keeping out of sight, which was more or less interesting. Here all I do is eat, sleep and kill time as best I can. I have been on crutches over a week now so of course I don't spend much daylight in bed. Was horribly weak at first and couldn't walk over thirty feet without a rest. A little exercise soon remedied that and since the first couple of days I've been going everywhere I want to (inside the building, of course. Too much snow outside for pajamas and carpet slippers) I am feeling fine and my hurts are improving steadily – I know that without being told. But I don't know any more about when I'll be out than you do. I asked doctors and nurses and head nurses, but none of them know and wouldn't tell you if they did. Which may be all right, but is not satisfactory.

The weather has been fine the last three days. Clear cold sunny days and moonlight nights.

We read and play cards and dominoes to kill time. Also make candy occasionally. We get cocoa, sugar, nuts and milk from the Red Cross and make fudge two or three times a week. It certainly is a great help. I have spent several hours lately working on the records, transferring individual records to the hospital books and vice versa. It affords me a change of occupation, which is very welcome, besides helping the nurses out. They are short of help here and the whole force is overworked.

I've written five pages and said nothing.
Will try to write oftener in future.

—Roy

(And probably I'll say even less.)

Sgt. R.E.Thompson 266969
Ward 280, B.H. 82
A.P.O. 784, A.E.F.

DIARY

Mon 10
Skin graft operation. No anesthetic. Very
sensational affair. This op. recommended
by Lt-Col who examined just previously.

Tue 11
Quiet day. Operation pronounced
successful by Lt. 11 new B. P. [bed patients]

Wed 12
Lots of excitement over B.P. train, which
failed to appear. No dressing. My back is
getting powerful sore. [The skin graft on Monday
the 10th was to help the much-operated-on stump heal.]

Thur 13
Both back and leg dressed today. Warmest
day for some time. Snow melting.

Fri 14
Leg dressed . Back better. Showery after
supper. Four men went to Nice.

Sat 15
Rainy. Learning to play 500. Played until
midnight.

Sun 16
Nothing to report.

TOUL, FRANCE, **2/16** *[1919]*

Dear Everybody back home:

It's a nice rainy Sunday afternoon, no good for writing letters or anything else. I intended to write Friday, but didn't get in the right mood, and yesterday the same. Today is no better but I'm going to see what I can do anyhow.

The past week has been the usual round of 3 meals and eight hours sleep daily. A trainload of patients left Tuesday, on their way home. They were certainly a happy gang. I'd feel a lot better if I knew when I would follow them. Things over here are certainly unsettled, but I expect a big move towards the U.S. before long.

I'm learning to play "Five hundred" Got into a game just after supper last night and played until nearly midnight. In the hospitals seems to be the only place where they don't gamble. Around the company nobody played cards, except Poker and Black Jack. I never played either, so this is the first cards I've played in some time.

The long cold spell is over. Began thawing Thursday and is raining pretty hard this afternoon. That makes things seem ever so much more natural, for when it isn't raining in this country you know something is wrong.

Had a big feed of fudge to-day. Material furnished by A.R.C.

This is enough trash, I guess.

Love to all of you,   — Roy

Sgt. R. E. Thompson 266969

280 W., B.H. 82, A.P.O. 784

American E. F.

DIARY

Mon Feb 17
Doctor cleaned my wound. It appears
to be working beautifully. Marked B.P.
again.

Tue 18
Doctors examining men. Rechecking B.P.
patients.

Wed 20
Robinson and 9 others B.P. [departed?]
Spring weather. Showery and sunny by
turns.

Thur 21
Filled up with new men. Business as usual.

Fri 22
Left B.H. 87 !!! Totally unexpected to
all of us. Anderson, Hilling and myself
from 280. Left Toul just before noon. Neuf
Chateau, Chaumont, Troyes.

Sat 23
Orleans, Vierzon, Chateauroux

Sun 24
Landed at Perigueux and Base 95 at 6:30
A.M. Very rainy.

Mon 25
Got my uniform. Outside for first time
since I was hurt.

Chapter 5

Coming Home

B.H. 95, Feb 25, 1919
[PERIGUEUX, FRANCE]

Dear Mother, Dad and the kids,

I don't know where I am, but am doing very well, thank you. Left Toul Saturday (22nd) about noon on a R.C. *[Red Cross]* train and got in here Monday morning. I've heard the name of the place a dozen times. It's plumb heathenish and I've entirely forgotten it. Anyway, it doesn't matter. I know I'm still in France because it's been raining ever since we got here.

Got a full new outfit this afternoon. Will be able to get outside occasionally now. Have been physically able for some time, but lacked wearing apparel, except pajamas, which are hardly suitable for sightseeing excursions in February. Have a whole new rig now, from the "cowhides and a keg of nails" on up.

The Red Cross has a fine place here, reading and writing rooms, library, canteen, etc. Three movie shows daily, two for patients and one for personnel. Think I'll go to-night and celebrate my liberty. It's sure a satisfaction to get outside again.

I like this place better than Toul, but I'm getting mighty tired of hospital life. I'd rather be with the boys and working than just killing time this way. Hope some mail comes soon. Haven't seen a letter for a month. The last ones were dated just after Christmas. Last I heard from

the co. they were still working, and no prospect of going home.
More when I have something to tell.

— Roy

Sgt. R.E.Thompson

B.H. 95, A.P.O. 794

DIARY

Wed Feb 26, 1919
Showery. Outside some. Chow is bum, but better than 82.

Thur 27
Wound entirely healed. No excitement except rumors of Bordeaux train.

Fri 28
Clear warm perfect day. Nothin' doin' !

Sat March 1
The same, excepts that it's raining cats and dogs.

Sun 2
Investigated the government educational system. A good time and some information.

Mon 3
Rainy. Rambled around camp and amused myself as usual.

Tue 4
Ditto. Going to mess hall for chow now. Doc allowed me to take a real bath.

PERIGUEUX   MAR 4, 1919

Dear Mother and Dad and the kids:

I've finally learned the name of this place. It is Perigueux, and it's about 50 miles from Bordeaux. I suppose you have the map I sent, so you can find it without trouble. They say it is one of the very oldest towns on France, which means that it has been here for some time. It is full of very old historic buildings. I would like to visit it, but don't suppose I'll have a chance.

I am going all over camp now, but can't go to town on crutches. I've been slipping out to the mess hall for dinner and supper, because I get more to eat that way, but continued to take breakfast in bed. I think they got wise to my graft today, so I'll probably have to get up for breakfast in the morning, which will be simply awful. Chow is good here, and we eat at tables with stuff put out in big dishes, home style, which I hadn't seen since Camp Lewis. French women do all the kitchen work. There is a small army of them around here, and they're sure a hard-looking crew.

I found a bathhouse to-day with real bathtubs, and even more wonderful, the place was clean. I had one wonderful bath. It was almost as good as Aix-les Bains.

This place is full of broken arms and legs. All fracture cases are going home now. We don't know when that will happen to us. I won't be surprised at sailing orders to-morrow or a month from to-morrow. Anyway, I'm ready. No mail yet, and don't expect any, after moving so much. It should follow, but doesn't seem to.

Love to all of you,

— Roy
Sgt. R. E. Thompson
B.H. 95, A.E.F.

DIARY

Fri 7
Dressings off for good. Hiked thru
cemetery with C.O.S. *[Commanding Officer
Surgery?]* A very interesting place.

Sat 8
Rained—Went to Red Cross show.

Sun 9
Showery. Nothing doing whatever.

Mon 10
Everything quiet. Warm, lovely day.

Tue 11
Another perfect day. Hear three trains
are coming soon.

Wed 12
Excitement beaucoup. All ready to move
at 5 P.M. Order cancelled. Supposed to
move in the morning.

Thur 13
Foggy morning. Loaded on R.C. train
immediately after breakfast. Reached
Beau Desert about 4 P.M.

Fri 14
Rainy. Nothing happening in particular.

Sat 15
Nice day. Very little rain. Went to head
office for classification. Made affidavits
on pay due.

Sun 16
Another nice day. Went to leg dept.
to be fitted. Office closed; going back
tomorrow. Wrote for my mail.

Mon 17
No rain. Making out sup. service records
and signing payroll. Beaucoup dances.

Tue 18
Went to leg dept. No luck. Came back and
had leg bandaged.

Beau Desert, France Mar 18, 1919

Dear Homefolks:

Well, how are things going to-day? This has been a lovely sunny day, but is clouding up this evening and will probably rain to-night. Yesterday we had a breeze off the ocean that felt just like a Chinook. It almost made me homesick.

We came down here Thursday, the 13th. Were all ready to move the preceding evening, but the train was late, so we didn't move until the next morning. This place is four miles from Bordeaux. Our train got here around 4 o'clock, I guess. And that same evening two Red Cross workers who had been sent here from Periguex a couple of days ahead of us, came over to see us. It seemed like meeting old friends, for they had been feeding us cookies and chocolate for two weeks, and we felt quite acquainted. Haven't been so lucky in finding the boys I know, tho. There are six or seven hospitals in this group, and I've never had time to go thru all of them. This is the last hospital to go thru before sailing, and nobody leaves until paid in full. If records are lost, supplementary records are made by affidavits. Payrolls are made the same way. Some of the fellows who came in after I did went out to-day. Guess it will be my turn soon. Here's hoping so, anyway.

I wrote for my mail the other day. Sent to the Central Post Office and having it sent home.

That's all. More some time.   — Roy

DIARY

Wed Mar 19
Beaucoup rain. Signed payroll A.M. Paid
in bed at 10:30 P.M.

Thur 20
Had cast made. Leg promised for
Saturday. Train in and ward filled up.

Fri 21
Such raining like neffer vas yet. Rained
all day.

Sat 22
[This was Roy's 23rd birthday]
Good day. Not much rain. Got my new

leg and hiked around some. Doesn't fit very well.

Sun 23
Showery. Took pneumonia shot. My leg fits better (due to whittling) and is almost usable. Stewart located me.

Mon 24.
Walking pretty well. Arm is stiff but not very sore.

Tue 25
Padded cast and it goes still better. Went to show, which was punk.

Wed 26
Got some insignia. B.H. 20 leaving and both our old nurses quit.

Thur 27
Two new nurses. Went to good show, 319th F.A. Sent $40 home.

B.H. 111 MARCH 27, 1919

Mine Honored Relatives:

As I believe I told you, I drew a few francs the other day, and I have decided I won't need them all. So I'm inclosing a money order for $40. You can buy chewing gum or carpet tacks or some other essential commodity with it. I'm not particular what, just so you have a good time.

Things are almost as exciting here as they were last week. We're still just lying around waiting for a boat, which is pretty monotonous business. I found my Spangle friend a few days ago, or rather, he found me and I see him quite often now. Took a shot Monday to prevent flu and pneumonia. Arm was stiff for about a day. Am feeling fine, and have discarded my crutches.

— Roy

Unlike the diary entries, Roy's letter doesn't mention being fitted with an artificial foot, he just says "...have discarded my crutches".

Diary

Fri Mar 28
Sunny. Slight infection. Wooden leg is resting today.

Sat 29
Rain and wind. Leg still resting.

Sun 30
Beaucoup wind and beaucoup rain. Wore leg some more. Another bunch getting ready to move to 20. [Base Hosp. 20]

Mon 31
Nearly froze last night. Snowing today. Went to school afternoon.

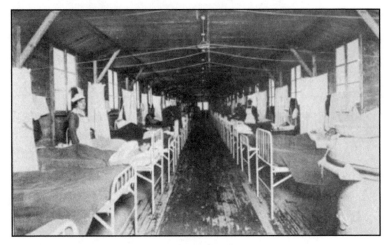

A typical WWI Army Hospital (ready for inspection)

Tue April 1
Went to school, thereby missing chance to
sign payroll. Stormy.

Wed 2
Clear fine day. Spent the afternoon trying
to get on the payroll. School afternoon.

BEAU DESERT 4/2 [1919]

Dear Homefolks:

This has been a nice sunny day and I had some R.C. ice cream
a few minutes ago so I feel pretty good to-night. The last five
days have been bad enough for March in the Palouse. All of them
windy and pouring rain, except Sunday when it snowed nearly
all day. Was a rotten cold day. To-day was lovely. I am going to
school now. Started day before yesterday. Am taking only Draft-

ing at present. Am more awkward at it than I had expected to be, so will be some time getting the knack of it again. Don't seem to have forgotten much of the little I knew, tho. I may take up another subject next week if I'm still here. Haven't quite decided yet. Anyway, it's a great thing to have something to occupy my time.

Beaucoup love to all of you,

— Roy

DIARY

Thurs April 3, 1919
School forenoon. Stayed at home after
[noon] to sign payroll. It came around
after chow but I didn't sign. Went to show.
Very good hypnotist.

Fri 4
Showery. School all day. Payroll signed at
noon.

Sat 5
School forenoon. Rambled over camp
after. New canteen opened in 114,
wherein I invested somewhat.

Sun 6
Went to church in E.H. 20. Long walk
afternoon, missing my chow.

Mon 7
School again. Rumors of leaving are
flying thick. Went to 319 M.A. show.

Beau Desert Hospital, Bordeaux

Tue 8
Giving my leg a rest, due to a blister.
Stayed at home all day for pay, but didn't
get it.

Wed 9
Stayed at home some more. Paid
afternoon @ 5.80. Drew francs 172.
Wearing my leg with little inconvenience.
Supposed to leave tomorrow.

Thur 10
Move postponed until Saturday. Had new
cast made. Went to school afternoon.

Fri 11
Got my new leg, but too soft to wear. Had
a little feed in Ward 4.

Sat 12
Loaded on H.T. 67 *[Hospital Train]* about
9 o'clock. Left 111 @ 11:30. Bordeaux,
Saintes, Rochefurt-sur-Nu.

Sun 13
Nantes, 1:30 AM Vannes, Auroy. Ran
all afternoon thru very pretty and
picturesque country. Reached Kerhuon
and Base *[hospital]* 65 before dark.

Mon 14
Trans. *[fer]* to different ward. Issuing new
equipment. Very rainy and windy.

Tue 15
Drew most of my new outfit. To be
inspected tomorrow. Lots of wind and
some rain.

Wed 16
Drew full equipment. Inspected afternoon
and papers made out.

Thur 17
Fine day. Wore new leg and getting along
fine. Men in from E.H. 20.

Fri 18
Another peach of a day. Litter patients
went out, O.B. among them.

Sat 19
Another perfect day. Spent afternoon on

Kerhuon Hospital

the beach. Got myself a drawing set. Going
to work some more.

Sun 20
Easter Sunday. Eggs for breakfast
and sweet potatoes for dinner. Most
remarkable occurrence in my army
experience. Fine weather.

Mon 21
More fine weather. Afternoon and evening
on the beach. Tagged after supper.
*[Obviously means "Stay close, you are about to be shipped
out!"]*

Tue 22
Stayed around ward all day waiting for
orders. No excitement.

Wed 23
*Receiving ward 8:30. Ambulance, dock,
lighter. U.S.S. President Grant. We were the
first to load.*

Thur 24
*Loading more 77th men and a few nurses.
Sailed about 3 P.M. Sea rather rough
and all feeling it. I have a prodigous
headache but didn't quite feed the fish.*

Fri 25
*Still headachy. Sea smoother than
yesterday. Some breeze.*

Sat 26
*Good weather and feeling better but not
very good yet.*

Sun 27
*A perfect day. Sea very smooth. Two ships
in sight, one all day.*

Mon 28
*Another trans [port] passed us early in the
morning, before I was up, in fact. Out
1084 miles at noon. Average speed 11.6
knots. Very warm.*

Tue 29
*Cooler than yesterday and a fresh breeze.
Getting a little rough afternoon. U.S.S.
Cape Finisterre [a troop transport] passed us.*

U.S.S. President Grant…..Roy E. Thompson returned home to New York City aboard this ship from Brest, France, April 24 to May 6, 1919

PRESIDENT GRANT SP-3014

The third ship named for Ulysses S. Grant was the former President Grant which was built in 1907 by Harland and Wolff, Ltd., Belfast, Ireland for the Hamburg American Packet Steamship Co. After several years of trans-Atlantic passenger service, she was interned at New York in 1914 and seized there on 6 April 1917 when the United States entered World War I. Turned over to the Navy, she was commissioned President Grant (SP-3014) on 2 August 1917, Comdr. J. P. Morton in command.

During her operations as a troop transport she made 16 round trips between New York and ports of France carrying a total of 40,104 servicemen on her eastbound passage, and a total of 37,025 servicemen on her westbound returns to New York. President Grant was transferred to the Army 6 October 1919.

Wed 30
Roughest day we have had. Nobody sick.
Beaucoup wind. New York 1506 miles.

Thur May 1
Much rougher than yesterday. Wind high,
went down afternoon. Some rain. Speed
8.6 knots.

Fri 2
Wind high and considerable sea. Head
wind. No rolling but considerable
pitching. Brest 2064. N.Y. 1064.

Sat 3
Much better weather. Shower apremidi.
G. Wash. and Arizona passed us 6:30 P.M.
Some fog. [This is battleship Arizona that was sunk at
Pearl Harbor, 1941]

Sun 4
Perfect day, warm and light breeze.
Smoothest sea I ever saw. Speeding up
since last night in order to get in Tues.
morn. in time for the 77th Division
Parade.

Mon 5
Foggy nearly all day. Considerable
whistling. Light breeze and smooth sea.
Colder.

Tue 6
Perfect day. Came into port just after

noon. Beaucoup boats out and a million
people. Docked at Hoboken, unloaded
on river boat, then to ambulance and to
D.H. 5. Bed about 11 P.M. after bath and
numerous inspections.

Wed 7
No clothes, hence no excitement. Ice
cream and strawberries for dinner.
Raided my barrack bag and rescued my
souvenirs.

Thur 8
Got my uniform and went out to see the
town with Green. Show after chow.

Fri 9
Robinson and wife came over. Had
dinner and went to Palace Theatre, where
$5,000,000 was raised for Victory Bonds.
Raining.

Sat 10
Raining again. Lambs Club*
took us to show, then the feed of our lives.
[* A private New York club for theatre performers and
musicians...formed in 1874.]

Sun 11
Bus ride over town. Went up Woolworth
Tower. S and S Club supper and a show.
More bus ride. Cool.

Mon 12
Lots of the boys leaving. Went motoring
afternoon to Bronx Park and over town.
After supper went for walk to 30ᵗʰ Street.

Tue 13
Moved to Gen. Hosp. 3 at Rahway, N.J. via
ambulance, ferry and train. Lovely warm
day. Don't fancy the camp very much.

Wed 14
Warm but cloudy. Went to school and
for examination. Trying to get a new
leg. Went to big dance at K.C. but didn't
indulge.

Thur 15
Showery evg. Went to N.Y. with intentions
of visiting Coney Island but desisted
owing to rain. Went out for dinner and a
play "Pretty Soft".

Fri 16
Stayed at home most of time. Hot day and
no excitement.

Sat 17
Hot. Thunder shower après midi. Nothing
of importance happened.

Sun 18
Swell day. Friends from N.Y. came out.
Good time.

Mon 19
Went to school and generally behaved
myself.

Tue 20
Rainy evg. Went to N.Y. and very
interesting time I had.

Wed 21
Met train in Rahway. Went to Rahway
movies. Very good time. Rainy.

Thur 22
Got Mamie's telegram. Wrote letters; also
replied by wire. Went to parish house party
in Elizabeth. It was hardly a success.

Fri 23
Went to very good show in Elizabeth.
Came back before chow. Went to Rahway
as requested by delayed wire. Big thunder
shower.

Sat 24
Thunder shower evg. Rose and Mary S.
came out for a little while.

Sun 25
Warm perfect day. Mary McC came out.
Very good time.

Mon 26
Still hot day. Went to Rahway evg. and to
movies.

Tue 27
School forenoon. 2:57 to New York, Hall of
States, rubberneck bus and Central Park.
Very good time.

Wed 28
Stayed at home and behaved myself.
School forenoon and afternoon. Hot,
sultry day.

Thur 29
Hot, sultry day. Got Mother's letter. Got
transfer orders. To be moved Saturday.

Fri 30
Big field day. Lots of doins; one-legged
football; water fight, baseball, etc.
Canteen after chow and spent evg.

Sat 31
Beautiful day, but hot. School forenoon.
After went to Bloomfield to ent.
[entertainment] and feed. Some feed too.
Visited big munitions plant.

Sun June 1
Beastly hot. All trips planned proved
failures. Went to canteen after chow.

Mon 2
Drew my money and made other
preparations for departure. Went to
Rahway and watched 2:49 train sail by.
Back to camp and then to N.Y.

Tue 3
Tried it again with better luck. Caught
2:49 train for Chi. by way of Philly and
Pittsburg. Very hot day.

Wed 4
Train late. Reached Chi 6:15. All
berths taken on 6:30 west. Went to R.C.
restaurant and Y hotel.

Thur 5
All Chi is getting ready for the big 33rd
Div. Parade today. Caught Pacific Ltd.
on Chi. And N.W. 10:30. Crossing Ill and
Iowa. Cooler weather.

Fri 6
Crossing Nebraska and Wyoming. Went
over highest point on the line (Sherman,
Wyo.)

Sat 7
Crossed Salt Lake and Nevada desert. Hot
and dusty.

Sun 8
Sierra Nevadas to coast. Cal. looks good to
me. Lovely day. Reached Letterman 4P.M.
and went to suspect ward.

Mon 9
Stayed in all day to see Dr. who came
about 4 P.M. Made out transfer to Ward 7.

Tue 10
Stayed in again. Went to clinic. Transfer
changed to Ward 4.

Wed 11
Other wards full. Went to Ward 26. Taking
up some more algebra.

[From Envelope]
SGT. ROY E. THOMPSON, WARD 26
LETTERMAN GENERAL HOSPITAL
PRESIDIO, SAN FRANCISCO, CAL.
FRISCO, JUNE 12 [1919]

Dear Everybody:

I guess it's time for me to get busy and write you a line or two.
I got out of the quarantine ward yesterday, but as I didn't get a pass
to-day I'm no better off as yet. I attended two clinics to-day; the

first a skin disease clinic. Was sent there because of a little heat rash on my leg. There wasn't a sign of it four or five days ago and probably won't be that number of days hence. It broke out the day we crossed the Utah desert. The next one was for some other purpose, -- just what I don't know, since they dismissed me immediately because I had no X-ray photograph. Suppose I will have one taken to-morrow. After the clinics I was sent to the laboratory, where they extracted something less than four gallons of blood from my arm for test purposes. Hope they satisfy themselves by discovering germs of known diseases only. There are plenty of those without having new ones discovered.

Got a couple of letters from Mamie to-day. You people seem to have the idea that I am coming home right away. I don't expect to be discharged for three or four months, but will get a furlough sooner; perhaps in a month. I hardly expect it sooner, considering the red tape that must be unwound. You have to tell when your great-great-grandfather died, and why, and what church he belonged to, and how much intoxicating liquor he used per annum, in order to get a pair of sox around here, and I suppose if I wanted a furlough I'd have to tell his exact age when he cut his first tooth. But, as I said before, I don't suppose I will be able to get a furlough for a month or six weeks, so a camping trip before harvest seems to me out of the question. By September, it seems to me, I should be able to come home for perhaps two months, one month, anyway. Even if I get a furlough soon, I probably couldn't get more than seven or ten days.

Of course, if you're worrying about my general health, I'll apply for a furlough immediately and see what can be done. But I don't believe I can get one for, as I said, a month or six weeks, and even if I could, am not sure that it would be best, much as I would like to see you.

Mamie says you are still worrying because you can't get definite information about my difficulty. Well, rest assured that it's the right leg only, and it's only four inches above the ankle, and the

Letterman Hospital, San Francisco, California

left one is worth any six legs in Whitman County. It's life size and full of pep. The distances it will propel me surprise even me. You asked about the X-ray I had in N.J. The report on it was written in language beyond my feeble powers. I tried to read it, but failed utterly. Suppose it was all right, tho, as nothing more was said about it.

I'm going to quit and study my algebra.

— Roy

DIARY

Thur June 12
Couldn't get pass. Attended two clinics.
Enrolled in Mechanical Dwg.

Fri 13
Trans. To Ward 4. Took X-Ray and
Wasserman test. Went to S.F. Had picture
taken and went to Lodge.

Sat 14
Went on 1 o'clock pass with Hering. Five of
us went to party; returned at 4 A.M.

Sun 15
4 A.M. - 6 A.M. played Pedro. Started for
San Jose eight o'clock. Thirty in truck.
Had trouble, arrived 2 P.M. Started
back at 5. Got home; had lunch and to
hospital. Got in 11:30.

Mon 16
Went to school. No excitement whatever.

Tue , Wed, Thur, 17 - 18 - 19
Ditto

Fri 20
Uncle Wm. [Thompson] appeared and I went
home with him. Went on train arriving 7
P.M. Had lots of trouble getting a pass to
get out.

Sat 21
[Santa Cruz, CA] Went fishing in the bay. No
luck whatever. P.M. down to the beach to
see the sights.

Sun 22
Left S.C. on 8:30 bus. Got in about noon.
Joy ride to San Mateo in the P.M.

Mon 23
My leg is improving wonderfully. Went to

*town and had my picture retaken. Went
to Casino Theatre "Oo La La".*

*Tue 24
School A.M. and P.M. No excitement
whatever.*

*Wed 25
The same, exactly.*

*Thur 26
Throat and wound cultures taken for
diph. Went to school and to town 3 P.M.*

*Fri 27
Trying to get furlough. No luck as yet.
Hope for better tomorrow.*

*Sat 28
Furlough approved by captain. Couldn't
find major. Went to town to "Shepherd of
the Hills". Everybody celebrating.* [Germany
signed Peace Treaty at Versailles this day.]

*Sun 29
Went motoring to Half Moon Bay and San
Mateo with Peters family. Very nice drive.*

*Mon 30
Inspection by major. Two weeks furlough
promised. Measured for Letterman leg. Got
pkg. from home.*

Tues July 1
Spent the day between school and trying
to hurry my furlough.

Wed 2
Chasing the furlough. Signed at 4 P.M.
Went to Oakland and had dinner with
Miss Clark.

These diary entries conclude Roy's story of his encounter with
World War I. We know that he returned to Letterman General
Hospital in January of 1920 to receive his discharge.

CHAPTER 6

Becoming

A

Civilian

Honorable Discharge from The United States Army

War Department,
The Adjutant General's Office,
Washington, March 18, 1920.

these items is erroneous.

[signature]
Adjutant General.

The records of this office show that this soldier's serial number is 266969, that he served as a member of 13th Co., 1st Air Service Mechanics, and was appointed a sergeant January 1, 1918, and that so much of the certificate as shows otherwise with regard to

360.99

TO ALL WHOM IT MAY CONCERN:

This is to Certify, That* _Roy E. Thompson (266969)_

† _Sergeant 13th Company A S M_

THE UNITED STATES ARMY, *as a* TESTIMONIAL OF HONEST AND FAITHFUL

SERVICE *is hereby* HONORABLY DISCHARGED *from the military service of the*

UNITED STATES *by reason of* _certificate of disability 3 S del & D dated Jan 20, 1920._

Said _Roy E. Thompson_ _was born_

_in_ _actions_ _, in the State of_ _Mich._

When enlisted he was _21½_ _years of age and by occupation a_ _mechanic._

He had _Blue_ _eyes,_ _Lt Brown_ _hair,_ _Ruddy_ _complexion, and_

was _5_ _feet_ _9_ _inches in height._

Given under my hand at _Letterman Gen'l Hospital Presidio S F Cal_ _this_

_28_ _day of_ _January_ _, one thousand nine hundred and_ _twenty_

[signature]

J. M. Kennecy,
Colonel Medical Corps.

Commanding.

*See amendment.

Form No. 525, A. G. O.
Oct. 9-18.

*Insert name, Christian name first; e. g., "John Doe."
† Insert Army serial number, grade, company and regiment or arm or corps or department; e. g., "1,620,302"; "Corporal, Company A, 1st Infantry"; "Sergeant, Quartermaster Corps"; "Sergeant, First Class, Medical Department."
‡ If discharged prior to expiration of service, give number, date, and source of order or full description of authority therefor.

9—4164

Honorable Discharge

Enlistment Record
Original On Back of Honorable Discharge

The "Enlistment Record" dated Jan 28, 1920, is a most telling piece of paper, bearing multiple rubber stamps with dates and names; the last being Jun 1, 1921. Roy was apparently still denying "Horsemanship", while the government had no documentation regarding his promotion to sergeant, or prophylaxis regard-

ing typhoid or paratyphoid. They did acknowledge that he was entitled to transit pay and a bronze victory button. I also extracted from this document an example of Roy's sense of humor. Notice, following "Character", the words "Very Good". Looks to me like his own handwriting!

Here is a Washington State record card of Roy's Veteran's Compensation Fund payment of $360. Warrant issued on June 7, 1921. This also confirms his dates of service, though this card is different from his application which lists Nov 4, 1917 (Colfax, Washington) and Jan 28, 1920 (Letterman General Hospital, San Francisco).

Without more letters or diary entries, the facts of his army life end.

An application for Equalization Compensation to the State of Washington was filed on Feb. 11, 1920. It states that he had been discharged on Jan 26, 1920, and reported a Washington State College dormitory as his permanent residence.

Before June of 1925 Roy had filed for a homestead in Okanogan county, Washington, and lived on it long enough to obtain title (six months). He rented the land to a local rancher for practically nothing for many years, and eventually sold it, probably in the 1950s.

In 1921 he completed his high school work in the special program at Washington State College at Pullman (now Washington State University). He then enrolled in a college course that led to two degrees in June of 1925....Bachelor of Science in Mechanical Engineering and Bachelor of Arts in Education.

Not all of Roy's time at Washington State was devoted to class work...as shown by the photos of him spoofing the military and sitting in his car.

From 1925 Roy worked as a mechanical engineer. His first position was with the United States Patent Office in Washington D.C. He left after a year and worked for a series of engineering manufacturing companies until he retired in 1968. He specialized in the design of gears and power transmission equipment and held at least two patents.

Roy married Hester McCracken in 1925. They had two children and four grandchildren.

Roy and Hester are buried in the cemetery at Pullman, Washington.

*Spoofing the
military…*

Roy's car . . . 1925

Roy and his mother Cora Thompson
On the occasion of his graduation from Washington State College,
June 1925

Addendum

The Letters

Autobiography

By: Roy E. Thompson

This was a high school English class assignment written in May 1921 during the one year of college preparatory study at Washington State College.

In looking back over my life I find but little which might interest the average reader. It is true that I have had a few experiences, which, had they occurred a few years earlier, might have been of some interest. Ten years ago a trip around the United States, not to mention a holiday excursion to France, was somewhat of a novelty. Three years ago these excursions were provided, with expenses paid, and so many young men took one or both trips that to do so excited no comment whatever.

To go back and begin at the beginning, I was born on a farm. My parents both grew up on farms and have no desire to live elsewhere or to engage in any other occupation. My grandparents were of hardy Scotch Irish pioneer stock, farming from necessity perhaps as much as from choice. My uncles, like my father, have without exception stayed on the farm. They have, however, shown a versatility somewhat unusual, which may account in some measure for their success. This versatility I have inherited, as did at least two of my cousins. These men, like myself, both grew up on a farm. Both, too, turned to mechanical work as being more congenial. In my case, this mechanical inclination showed itself very early in life. Almost as soon as I could lift a hammer I was trying to build things, and my affection for the inside of watches and alarm clocks was disastrous to their time-keeping qualities. During my school days this inclination had little chance to develop. I worked on the farm, learning farming as all boys do who grow up under such conditions, and at sixteen I could turn my hand with fair success to any job on the farm. I learned to handle horses fairly well, and tho my father had several fine ones, I never cared for them. My liking for machinery grew constantly greater instead of less, and I began reading on the subject. My father was deeply disappointed that I did not care for farming, but was too broad-minded to blame me. Instead he provided me with such books as I wished, saying, "It's no use spoiling a good mechanic to make a poor farmer." After finishing the grades, I did not attend school again for four years. I realized that I knew much more than most people needed to know, so why bother about school? About three years after I left school, I worked thru a winter in a garage. Here I was much surprised to learn that I knew nothing about electricity. When I started to read on the subject, I was amazed to run across algebraic formulas. This I could not understand. What business had a foolish subject like algebra to get mixed up with electricity, anyway. The discovery, when I recovered from the shock, showed me that I should go to school some more. This I did the following winter. I found then that high school subjects were not so foolish as I had thot, and I decided to continue. The winter immediately following, work prevented me from entering school again, but the second I began school work in September and finished the term. This was in May, 1917.

That autumn I found myself in training camp, very busily wearing out Uncle Sam's hob-nailed shoes. Not for long, tho, for February found me in France. That summer of 1918 was somewhat eventful; the winter decidedly dreary. In May of 1919 I again saw the Statue of Liberty, but I was not discharged from the Army until January of 1920.

Last fall I entered the Department of Elementary Science of the State College of Washington from which I hope to graduate this year. And I also hope that in 1925 I will receive my diploma from the College of Engineering.

My experiences and observations have brot about some very decided changes in my opinion of education. From complete satisfaction over an eighth grade diploma to a great desire for all the education I can get is a considerable reversal of sentiment. I am indeed thankful that I was shown the advantages of education before all opportunity of acquiring one was gone.

In summing up, it seems to me that this change of ideas will probably do more towards shaping my future than any other event. My autobiography is now certainly not worth writing, and if at any future time it should prove to be, education will be responsible for the change. I sincerely hope that I may find opportunity to do something which will be of more interest to the world than anything I have so far accomplished.

Roy's "Identity Discs" ("Dog Tags" in WWII and later")

Identity Discs Become Standard Issue for Soldiers in WWI.

By the 1890's the US Army and Navy began experimenting with issuing metal identification tags to recruits. During WWI, the French wore a bracelet with a metal disk, called a plaque d'identité, that was engraved with the soldier's name, rank and formation. (from www.agilewriter.com/History/DogTags.htm)

When the United States entered the war in 1917, all soldiers were issued two aluminum tags that were hand-stamped with their name, rank, serial number, unit and religion. The tags were suspended from their necks by cord or tape.

Roy's identity discs were in his box of "old army stuff". These were made sometime after January 10, 1918; in that letter he says, "To-morrow we each get a number." The first letter where he asked to have the number included as part of his address is dated December 23, 1918, six weeks after the armistice! The tags show both "S C" for Signal Corps. and "AIR SERVICE". The explanation is that the Air Service was part of the Signal Corps.

CAMPS, TOWNS AND HOSPITALS MENTIONED
IN ROY'S LETTERS AND DIARIES

Fort Lewis, Washington

Kelley field No. 1, San Antonio, TX

Camp Hancock, Agusta, GA

Camp Merritt,

Out on the Atlantic

St. Nazaire (Landed 26 Feb 1918)

Langres, France

Abainville, France

Aix les Bains

Dijon

Lyon

St. Mihiel

Sampigny, Meuse

Blois

Gondrecourt

Langres, Haute Marne

Canal Tunnel, Near Houdlaincourt

Toul (Base Hospital 95)

Toul (BH. 82)

Verdun

Commercy

Perigueux (50 miles from Bordeaux)

Beau Desert (4 miles from Bordeaux)

Brest, France (departure for N.Y.)

D.H. 5

Gen. Hosp. 3 (Rahway, New Jersey)

New York

Chicago

San Francisco

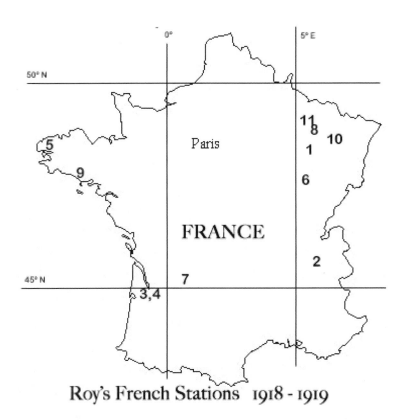

Roy's French Stations 1918 - 1919

1	Abainville	Apr/May/Jun 1918	48.53N/5.5E
2	Aix les Bains	Sept 24 –Oct 5, 1918	45.70N/5.92E
3	Beau Desert	March 13, 1919	44.83N/0.56W
4	Bordeaux	April 12, 1919	44.83N/0.56W
5	Brest to New York	Apr 24 -May 6, 1919	48.4N/4.5W
1	Gondrecourt, Meuse	Jan 5 - 28, 1919	48.52N/5.5E
6	Langres, Haute Marne	July 1, 1918	47.51N/5.1E
7	Perigueux B.H. 95	February 24, 1919	45.18N/0.72E
8	Sampigny	November 1, 1918	48.8N/5.52E
9	St. Nazaire, France	February 24, 1918	47.28N/2.2W
10	Toul B.H 45 and B.H 87 (82 ?)	January 28, 1919	48.68N/5.9E
1	Tunnel on Meholle Canal	July 21, 1918	48.6N/5.5E
11	Verdun (Verdun-sur-Meuse)	December 1, 1918	49.17N/5.38E

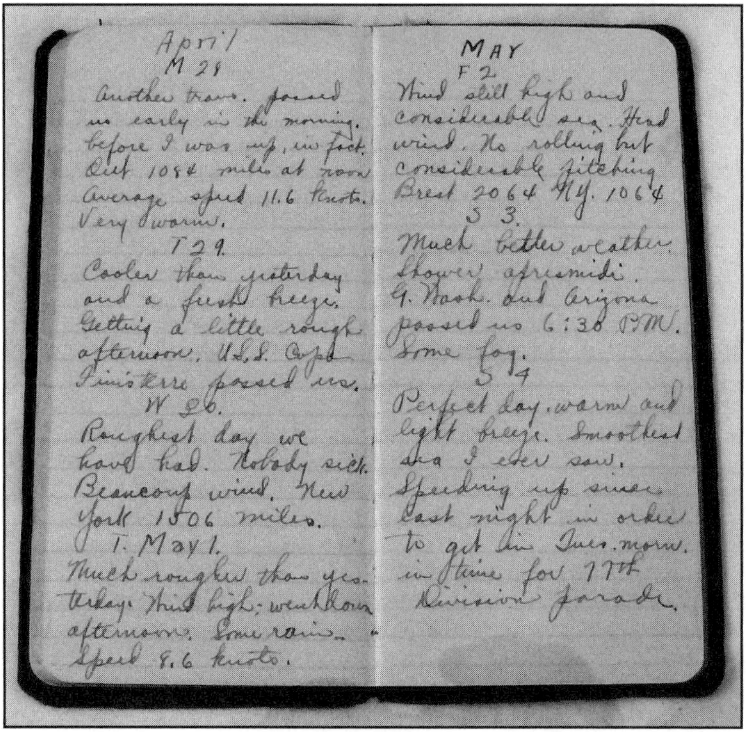

April
M 28
Another trans. passed
us early in the morning,
before I was up, in fact.
Out 1084 miles at noon
Average speed 11.6 knots.
Very warm.
T 29.
Cooler than yesterday
and a fresh breeze.
Getting a little rough
afternoon. U.S.S. Cape
Finistere passed us.
W 30.
Roughest day we
have had. Nobody sick.
Beaucoup wind. New
York 1506 miles.
T. May 1.
Much rougher than yes-
terday. Wind high; went down
afternoon. Some rain.
Speed 8.6 knots.

MAY
F 2
Wind still high and
considerable sea. Head
wind. No rolling but
considerable pitching
Brest 2064 N.Y. 1064
S 3.
Much better weather.
Shower apresmidi.
G. Wash. and Arizona
passed us 6:30 PM.
Some fog.
S 4
Perfect day, warm and
light breeze. Smoothest
sea I ever saw.
Speeding up since
last night in order
to get in Tues. morn.
in time for 77th
Division parade.

The Diaries